The Solitude Edge

HARNESSING SOLITUDE FOR SUCCESS AND GROWTH

Padmaraj PJ

Dedication

To the rebels, the dreamers, and the quiet explorers of life—this book is for you.

It's not a rulebook or a blueprint. It's a reminder that the world's noise doesn't define you and that solitude isn't loneliness; it's a forge. In your stillness, you can discover the courage to ask the right questions, the strength to hold your own, and the clarity to choose your path—one that feels right to you, not to everyone else.

This is your green light to pause, reflect, and grow on your own terms. To stop waiting for permission from people who don't walk in your shoes. To embrace the quiet moments and let them be the fuel for something greater.

Take this as a heartfelt nudge. A reminder. A friendly push. The power to unlock your next chapter isn't out there, waiting for someone else's approval. It's in here, inside you. All you have to do is trust it.

Now is your time. Go.

With gratitude,
Padmaraj PJ

Contents

Foreword

If you're like most people, you've been taught to avoid solitude—like it's some quiet monster lurking in the shadows, ready to pounce on your peace of mind. Society's unofficial motto could be summed up as "the busier, the better." A packed social calendar is celebrated; a night alone with your thoughts, not so much. But what if that's all wrong?

Here's the radical idea: solitude isn't your enemy. It's your secret weapon.

Rethinking Solitude

Picture this: some of the most brilliant minds in history—think Buddha, Einstein, Tesla, Steve Jobs—didn't stumble upon their breakthroughs in the midst of constant noise and distractions. They found clarity in the quiet. They uncovered insights in the stillness. They knew that solitude wasn't about loneliness; it was about focus, about tuning out the noise so they could hear their own inner genius.

What if you could do the same?

The Shift You Didn't See Coming

The modern world seems almost allergic to quiet. We're bombarded by pings, posts, and endless content that keeps our minds revving at full speed. It's no wonder that many of us equate stillness with discomfort. But here's the thing: if you can't be alone with your own thoughts, who's really in control—your mind or the distractions you feed it?

Let that sink in for a moment. If your sense of calm relies on constant external stimuli, what happens when it's just you and your thoughts?

A New Way Forward

This book isn't a guide to becoming a hermit or living off the grid. It's about taking back your mind. It's about turning solitude into a source of strength, creativity, and mental clarity. By the time you finish these pages, you'll see solitude not as a void, but as a vast, untapped resource for transformation.

Here's what you'll discover:

- How solitude can spark creativity and unlock insights you didn't know you had
- Why being comfortable alone is the ultimate act of emotional resilience
- How focusing deeply, without distractions, leads to extraordinary success
- And how every meaningful relationship—including the one with yourself—improves when you truly know who you are

But above all, this book will help you realize that you don't need to be surrounded by people to feel whole. You're already complete.

So, let's dive in. See what happens when you embrace solitude. You might just find that the edge you've been searching for was within you all along.

Preface

There's a moment we all experience—when the laughter fades, the calls go unanswered, and the world feels eerily silent. It's in that silence where loneliness seeps in, wrapping itself around us like a heavy fog.

For some, solitude becomes a cruel mirror, reflecting self-doubt and isolation. But for others, solitude is something else entirely—a quiet space where strength is cultivated, where purpose is realized, and where clarity takes root.

I know what it means to feel disconnected, to sit in a room and wonder if anyone truly understands. But I also know what happens when solitude is embraced as a powerful force for growth.

This book is not about escaping loneliness—it's about transforming it. It's about seeing solitude as an ally rather than an adversary.

Through these pages, you will discover how solitude can be the foundation of self-discovery, creativity, and success. **Each chapter offers insights, strategies, and structured exercises** designed to help you not only accept alone time but harness it as a tool to reshape your life.

By the end, my hope is that you no longer see solitude as something to fear but as something to nurture.

You are not alone in feeling lonely—but you do have the power to turn solitude into your greatest advantage.

Let's begin.

Acknowledgements

Every page of this book is woven together from lessons learned in solitude, conversations had in the quiet corners of life, and the wisdom of voices who never knew their words would reach me. It's not invention—it's transformation: reshaping decades of guidance, trial, and reflection into something deeply personal.

To the philosophers, thinkers, and authors whose works became my guides: your insights were the bread crumbs I followed when I felt lost. You showed me that what we often call "new" is simply an old truth rediscovered.

To the moments of stillness—those rare stretches of silence where my mind settled enough to hear something deeper—thank you for grounding me. Without you, the lessons of this book would have remained scattered, unexamined.

To the skeptics who questioned my direction, you gave me the push I needed to truly listen to myself. What began as doubts became the fire that shaped my resolve. Solitude showed me that validation is fleeting, but self-assurance is enduring.

To my family and friends: your understanding and support meant everything. I know my retreat into solitude was not always easy to watch, and I'm endlessly grateful that you allowed me the space to find my way.

And finally, to you—the reader: I hope these pages feel less like a set of instructions and more like a quiet conversation. If there's anything

I've learned, it's that the answers we seek are never far. Often, they're right where we least expect them—within us, patiently waiting for the moment we're ready to see them.

Prologue

"In solitude, the mind gains strength and learns to lean upon itself."

– Laurence Sterne

We live in a world that equates busyness with success and social validation with self-worth. From the endless notifications pinging on our phones to the unspoken pressure to always have plans lined up, we've been conditioned to believe that being alone is something to avoid, that silence is uncomfortable, and that happiness is found in the presence of others.

But what if everything you've been told about solitude is wrong?

What if being alone isn't a weakness, but a superpower?

Throughout history, some of the greatest minds—from Buddha meditating under the Bodhi tree to Nikola Tesla working late into the night—understood one fundamental truth: **solitude is not loneliness. Solitude is mastery.**

This book is not about isolating yourself from the world. It's about learning to thrive in your own company, unlocking your true potential, and using solitude as a tool for personal transformation.

Why This Book Matters Now More Than Ever

In the age of endless distractions, notifications, and constant connectivity, we've lost touch with the art of being alone.

We scroll through social media, consume an endless stream of content, and surround ourselves with noise—yet we still feel disconnected. We crave external validation, but rarely stop to ask ourselves:

Who am I when no one is watching?

This book is a journey toward answering that question.

You'll learn how to:

- **Transform solitude into a tool for creativity, focus, and self-awareness**
- **Rewire your mind to embrace being alone without feeling lonely**
- **Develop deep self-discipline and emotional resilience**
- **Harness mindfulness, visualization, and journaling for powerful inner growth**
- **Create a life where solitude becomes a strength—not a struggle**

How to Read This Book

This is not a book you simply read—it's a book you experience.

Each chapter is designed to challenge the way you think about solitude and provide practical exercises to help you integrate these lessons into your daily life.

By the end of this journey, you will no longer see solitude as something to escape. Instead, you'll embrace it as a powerful force for self-discovery, success, and inner peace.

Because once you master solitude, you master yourself.

Welcome to a new way of thinking.

01

The Power of Solitude

"Be like a tree and let the dead leaves drop."

— Rumi

What If Everything You Knew About Being Alone Was a Lie?

Let's get one thing straight.

You've been brainwashed.

Society taught you that being alone is bad. That if you're not constantly connected—texting, meeting up, or scrolling through social media—something must be wrong. You've been fed the idea that solitude = loneliness. That people who spend time alone are weird, antisocial, or even broken.

But here's the truth:

The ability to be alone is your superpower.

And the people who master solitude?

They become unstoppable.

Steve Jobs took long solo walks before making his biggest decisions.

Nikola Tesla locked himself in a room to invent technology that changed the world.

Buddha sat under a tree alone for 49 days—and emerged enlightened.

These weren't flukes. They knew something most people don't.

Solitude isn't the absence of connection—it's the foundation of it.

Because when you can sit in silence—when you can strip away the noise and distractions—you finally meet the one person who has the power to change everything.

Yourself.

The Great Misconception: Solitude vs. Loneliness

Most people fear being alone because they don't understand the difference between solitude and loneliness.

Loneliness is a craving for connection that goes unmet. It's that feeling of emptiness, like being in a crowded room and still feeling invisible.

Solitude, on the other hand, is a chosen state of being alone without feeling lonely. It's about presence, clarity, and self-discovery.

The difference?

Loneliness feels like isolation.

Solitude feels like power.

The problem is, most people have never been taught how to be alone.

When they find themselves in solitude—without a screen to distract them, a person to validate them, or noise to drown out their thoughts—they panic.

They reach for their phone. They binge-watch Netflix. They seek out pointless conversations just to avoid sitting in their own mind.

But here's the thing: If you can't be alone with yourself, you'll never truly know yourself.

And if you don't know yourself, how can you expect to build a life that actually makes you happy?

Why Solitude is Your Superpower

Think about it.

When was the last time you had a moment of absolute clarity—when everything suddenly made sense?"

Sitting by a window, watching the world go by?

Driving alone with no music, just lost in thought?

Flipping through an old journal and seeing your own growth?

That's no coincidence.

When you remove distractions, your brain shifts gears. It stops reacting and starts creating.

Here's what happens when you embrace solitude:

- **Your Mind Clears Up** – Mental noise disappears, and your thoughts become sharper.
- **Creativity Skyrockets** – Your subconscious starts making unexpected connections.
- **You Become Emotionally Stronger** – Because you no longer rely on others to validate you.
- **Decisions Get Easier** – Your gut instinct becomes your best advisor.

And here's the kicker—science backs this up.

Harvard research shows that solitude activates the Default Mode Network (DMN) in your brain. This is the system responsible for:

- Deep thinking
- Creative problem-solving
- Self-reflection and insight

This is why Bill Gates takes "Think Weeks" where he isolates himself to generate breakthrough ideas.

It's why some of the greatest minds in history chose solitude as a strategy.

But if solitude is so powerful, why do most people avoid it?

Because they've never been taught how to use it.

Let's change that.

The 3-Step Process to Unlock the Power of Solitude

Most people feel uncomfortable in solitude because they've never trained for it.

But just like going to the gym, your ability to be alone is a muscle. The more you practice it, the stronger you become.

Here's how to start—today:

1. The Five-Minute Reset

Most people can't sit still for five minutes without reaching for their phone.

So, let's rewire that.

Challenge: Spend 5 minutes today doing absolutely nothing.

No phone. No music. No distractions. Just sit, breathe, and let your thoughts flow.

At first, your mind will resist.

"This is boring."

"I should check my notifications."

"I need to be doing something productive."

Ignore it.

You're training your brain to handle stillness.

By Day 7, you'll notice something weird: You'll actually start craving these moments of silence.

2. Silence as a Daily Practice

You don't need to disappear into a cave to experience solitude.

But you do need to carve out space for pure silence.

Try this: Pick a 30-minute window today where you consume ZERO external input.

No social media.

No background noise.

No podcasts or music.

It will feel unnatural at first.

Then it will feel freeing.

3. Create a Solitude Ritual

Solitude isn't about doing nothing. It's about using that time intentionally.

Find a ritual that helps you connect with yourself:

- **Journal** – Write whatever comes to mind. Ideas, emotions, insights.
- **Take a solo walk** – No phone, no music. Just you and your thoughts.
- **Create something** – Paint, write, compose.

You don't have to overthink it. Just start.

Final Thoughts: Your Journey Starts Now

The people who master solitude?

They become unshakable.

They create. They innovate. They lead.

And if you commit to just five minutes a day, you'll start to notice:

- You think clearer.
- You feel calmer.
- You stop needing validation from others.

Solitude isn't about withdrawing from life. It's about stepping into your own power.

* * *

02

The Science of Solitude

"The quieter you become, the more you are able to hear."

— Rumi

What If Your Brain Needs Solitude as Much as It Needs Sleep?

Here's something that might surprise you:

Your brain is wired for solitude.

Not just in a "you need some downtime" way—more like a built-in, biological need that goes back to survival itself. And yet, modern life has conditioned us to run from being alone. From the moment we wake up, we're bombarded with notifications, emails, group chats, and videos.

We live in a world that worships noise.

But what if that noise is the very thing keeping you from your greatest ideas, insights, and potential?

When you strip away the distractions, your brain shifts gears. It rewires itself. It taps into creativity and focus in ways you can't access when you're constantly plugged in.

And the best part? Science proves it.

The Default Mode Network: Your Brain's Hidden Power

There's a system in your brain that comes alive when you're not busy reacting to external distractions. It's called the **Default Mode Network (DMN)**. This network handles:

- **Deep thinking** – Helping you process complex problems.
- **Creativity** – Making unexpected, groundbreaking connections.
- **Self-reflection** – Understanding who you are and what truly matters.
- **Memory consolidation** – Strengthening what you've learned and know.

Think of the DMN as your brain's backstage crew. When the noise dies down, it gets to work behind the scenes, organizing thoughts and sparking ideas. That's why your best epiphanies often strike not while working, but when you're:

- **In the shower**
- **On a quiet walk**
- **Staring out a window**

In these moments of stillness, your brain isn't idle. It's active, sorting through ideas, making connections, and unlocking insights you couldn't force to the surface.

The Neuroscience of Solitude: How Alone Time Rewires Your Brain

1. Your Brain Cleans Out Mental Clutter

Imagine your brain as a cluttered desktop with too many tabs open. Each notification and task add to the chaos. Solitude closes the unnecessary tabs. It files away the information you need, clears out what you don't, and creates room for new ideas.

- **Research from Harvard** shows that time spent alone triggers "neural consolidation." Your brain strengthens important memories, filters distractions, and primes itself for future growth.

Action Step: Take 10 minutes today to sit quietly. Just notice how your mind shifts from noise to clarity.

2. Solitude Supercharges Creativity

Scientists from the **University of California** found that mind-wandering—something that happens naturally in solitude—boosts creative thinking.

That's why figures like Nikola Tesla, Isaac Newton, and Steve Jobs intentionally used alone time to generate breakthrough ideas.

Your biggest "aha" moments don't happen when you're forcing yourself to think harder. They emerge when your conscious mind steps aside and your subconscious takes over.

Action Step: Next time you're stuck, don't force it. Step away for 15 minutes. Let your mind wander, and see what new ideas surface.

3. Alone Time Builds Emotional Strength

Most people avoid solitude because it forces them to face their fears, self-doubt, and unresolved emotions. But that's the very reason solitude is so powerful.

Studies show that individuals who regularly spend time alone build higher emotional resilience. They develop self-awareness and experience greater life satisfaction.

Action Step: The next time you feel uncomfortable alone, ask yourself:

- What am I afraid of facing?
- What thoughts am I avoiding?

Sit with that discomfort. That's where real growth begins.

How to Train Your Brain for Solitude (3-Step Method)

1. The 10-Minute Solitude Reset

Spend just 10 minutes a day in silence.

No phone. No distractions. Just you and your thoughts.

By the end of a week, you'll notice a shift—your mind will start craving these moments.

2. The Digital Detox Block

Set aside one hour each day to fully unplug.

No social media, no screens, no background noise.

This resets your brain's natural rhythm, allowing it to process emotions, clarify ideas, and recharge.

3. Create a "Think Space"

Choose a specific place—a chair, a park bench, a quiet corner—where you go to think.

Make it a habit. Over time, your brain will associate that space with clarity, focus, and creativity.

Your Move

Most people will never experience the full potential of their minds—because they never give it the space to breathe.

They smother it in noise.

They fill every moment with distractions.

They never let it do what it's designed to do: create, evolve, and inspire.

But you don't have to be most people.

Solitude isn't isolation—it's an upgrade.

And it starts now.

03

The 12-Step Roadmap to Harnessing Solitude

"Almost everything will work again if you unplug it for a few minutes, including you."

– Anne Lamott

* * *

Why Most People Fail at Solitude (And How You Won't)

Let's be real:

Most people don't fail at solitude because they hate it. They fail because they don't know how to handle it.

They sit down alone, feel a little uncomfortable, and then sprint back to their phones, their Netflix queues, or whatever noise they can find. And then they convince themselves, "Solitude just isn't for me."

But here's the thing: solitude isn't about sitting quietly doing nothing. It's about learning how to rewire your mind, to turn alone time into a superpower.

And like any superpower, it needs a system.

This 12-step roadmap is designed to take you from feeling uncomfortable with solitude to mastering it as a source of creativity, clarity, and power.

* * *

THE 12-STEP ROADMAP

Phase 1: Breaking Free from Distraction (Steps 1-4)

Phase 2: Rewiring Your Mindset (Steps 5-8)

Phase 3: Turning Solitude into Power (Steps 9-12)

Let's dive in.

* * *

PHASE 1: Breaking Free from Distraction

Step 1: The 5-Minute Solitude Habit

Start small. Most people can't go five minutes without reaching for their phone, so that's the first test.

Action Step: Today, spend five uninterrupted minutes in silence.

- No phone.
- No notifications.
- No music.
- Just you and your thoughts.

At first, it might feel unbearable. But if you can get through a week, you'll notice your mind starts to crave these moments of quiet.

Step 2: Block Out "No Input" Time

Your brain is overstimulated. You're constantly consuming information—emails, social media, podcasts, videos.

Action Step: Block out one hour a day where you consume ZERO external input.

- No screens.
- No talking.
- No music or podcasts.
- This is your detox window.

Step 3: Replace Noise with Thought

When you remove distractions, you might panic: "What do I do now?"

Solution: Replace the mindless input with intentional thinking.

- Instead of scrolling, journal.
- Instead of listening to music, take a silent walk.
- Instead of watching TV, meditate.

Step 4: Master the Art of Saying No

The biggest killer of solitude isn't your phone—it's overcommitting. Every time you say "yes" to something you don't truly want, you're saying "no" to yourself.

Action Step: Before saying "yes" to any invitation or request, ask:

- Does this align with what I truly want?
- Am I saying yes out of obligation or fear?
- If the answer doesn't serve you, say "no."

* * *

PHASE 2: Rewiring Your Mindset

Step 5: Reframe Solitude as Power, Not Loneliness

Your perspective shapes your reality.

New Reframe: Instead of thinking, "I'm alone," say, "I'm giving myself space to grow."

Step 6: Use Solitude to Train Your Intuition

Your gut instinct needs silence to speak.

Action Step: Next time you're faced with a big decision, sit in silence and listen to your gut instead of running to others for advice.

Step 7: Build Emotional Resilience in Solitude

Most people avoid being alone because they fear their own thoughts.

Truth: If you can't sit with your emotions, they control you.

Action Step: When uncomfortable thoughts surface, write them down. Process them. Let them pass. This practice will make you emotionally stronger.

Step 8: Shift from Consuming to Creating

Creativity thrives in solitude.

The Rule: Spend more time creating than consuming.

- Journaling > Scrolling
- Writing > Watching
- Thinking > Reacting

* * *

PHASE 3: Turning Solitude into Power

Step 9: Design Your Ideal Solitude Ritual

What makes you feel most connected to yourself?

- Journaling?
- Meditation?
- Silent walks?
- Pick one activity and commit to it daily.

Step 10: Create a "Think Space"

Choose a specific place where you go to think. Over time, your brain will associate this spot with focus and clarity.

Step 11: Embrace the Silence

Silence isn't empty—it's full of answers.

Practice: Spend at least 10 minutes a day in complete silence. No music, no podcasts, no distractions.

Step 12: Master the Balance Between Solitude & Social Life

Solitude doesn't mean isolating yourself. It means knowing when to connect and when to step back.

Rule: Choose your social interactions intentionally. Spend time with others because you want to—not because you feel obligated.

* * *

Final Thoughts: Your Move

Most people never unlock their mind's true potential because they never give it the space it needs to thrive. They drown it in distractions and deny it the time it requires to create and innovate.

But not you.

You have the roadmap. You have the system. Now it's up to you to use it.

Follow these 12 steps for 30 days, and you'll notice something incredible:

- Your mind will clear.
- Your creativity will explode.
- Your decision-making will sharpen.
- Your emotional strength will rise.

Most people will never master solitude. But you? You're different.

* * *

04

Breaking Free From External Validation

"Care about people's approval and you will always be their prisoner."

– Lao Tzu

* * *

What If Everything You Believe About Success Is a Lie?

Imagine waking up tomorrow without a single thought about what others think of you.

No pressure to impress.

No need to explain.

No craving for likes, praise, or approval.

How would your life change?

Would you chase the same goals?

Dress the same way?

Care about the same things?

Now here's the uncomfortable truth:

Most of what you do isn't for you.

You do it for how it will be perceived.

You do it because society rewards conformity.

You do it because somewhere along the way, you were taught that your worth is measured by how others see you.

But here's the thing:

The people who change the world don't seek validation. They reject it.

And solitude is your training ground for this shift.

Because when you master solitude, you stop needing external approval and start trusting your own internal guidance.

And those changes everything.

* * *

The Prison of Approval: Why You Care So Much

Thousands of years ago, being rejected by the tribe meant death. If you didn't belong, you didn't survive.

That's why your brain is terrified of disapproval—it still thinks you need acceptance to live.

But here's the thing: **this fear is outdated.**

You don't need permission to be yourself.

You don't need external validation to be worthy.

You don't need anyone's approval to thrive.

And yet, most people live trapped in this invisible prison—building their identities around what will get them accepted.

* * *

How Society Programs You to Seek Approval

From birth, you were taught a dangerous lie:

- **"Be a good boy/girl."** (Translation: Do what pleases others.)
- **Grades define your intelligence.** (Translation: Your worth is a number.)
- **Fit in or be left out.** (Translation: Never stand out.)
- **Success equals recognition.** (Translation: You only matter if others think you do.)

This programming is so deep you don't even realize how much of your life revolves around seeking approval.

Think about it:

- The job you took because it "sounded impressive."
- The clothes you bought because they "fit the image."
- The opinions you adopted because they "kept the peace."

The moment you start living for approval, you lose yourself.

Solitude is the way back.

* * *

The 3-Stage Process to Break Free from External Validation

If you want to stop caring about what others think, follow these three stages:

1. **Awareness** – Spot the hidden approval traps.
2. **Deconditioning** – Rewire your mind to detach from validation.
3. **Internal Mastery** – Learn to trust your own path.

Stage 1: Awareness – Identifying Where You Seek Approval

Step 1: The Brutal Truth Exercise

Ask yourself this:

If no one could ever see your success, would you still want it?

- Would you want that fancy job if no one knew what you did?

- Would you chase wealth if no one could see it?
- Would you care about looking perfect if no one was watching?

If the answer is "no," then you've just uncovered a part of yourself that exists purely for external validation.

Action Step: Write down five things you do for approval—not because you genuinely want them. This may surprise you.

Stage 2: Deconditioning – Rewiring Your Mind to Stop Seeking Validation

Step 2: Learn to Disappoint People (And Be Okay with It)

Here's the truth:

The more you grow, the more people you'll disappoint.

If no one is judging you, you're probably still playing small.

If no one disagrees with you, you're probably afraid to be real.

If no one is uncomfortable with your choices, you're probably following the script.

New Rule: Stop fearing disappointment. Start fearing a life that isn't yours.

Step 3: Reprogram Your "Why"

Most people chase goals because of how they'll be perceived—not because they actually want them.

Ask yourself:

- Do I want to be rich, or do I want to be seen as rich?
- Do I want success, or do I want others to think I'm successful?
- Do I want happiness, or do I want others to think I'm happy?

Action Step: Write down your biggest goal. Then ask:

"Would I still want this if no one could see it?"

If not, it's not your goal—it's society's. Let it go.

Stage 3: Internal Mastery – Trusting Your Own Path

Step 4: Build Self-Validation Rituals

External validation fades. Self-validation lasts.

- Instead of waiting for praise, list your own wins every day.
- Instead of seeking approval, remind yourself you're already enough.
- Instead of needing applause, celebrate your own progress.

Action Step: Every morning, write:

1. One thing you're proud of.
2. One thing you're grateful for.
3. One thing you're working on.

This trains your brain to look inward for validation.

* * *

Final Thoughts: The End of Approval-Seeking

Here's the ultimate test:

Are you living for yourself, or for the imaginary audience in your head?

Spoiler: They don't care.

Most people are too busy worrying about their own lives to constantly judge yours.

So stop performing for an audience that doesn't exist.

You never needed their approval.

You were free all along.

* * *

05

Building Emotional Resilience

"You don't have to control your thoughts. You just have to stop letting them control you."

– Dan Millman

* * *

The Lie You Were Told About Your Emotions

Let's get one thing straight:

Your emotions are not the problem.

The problem is how you've been conditioned to deal with them.

Most people grow up hearing one of two approaches to emotions:

1. **Suppress them.** "Stay strong. Don't let them show."
2. **Avoid them.** "Distract yourself—it'll pass."

When these approaches fail, people turn to numbing agents: food, social media, alcohol, work, mindless entertainment.

But here's the truth no one tells you:

If you can't sit alone with your emotions, they own you.

Mastering solitude isn't just about being physically alone—it's about handling what arises when you are. When you remove distractions, something uncomfortable happens. All the feelings you've been avoiding? They show up.

- **Self-doubt.**
- **Regret.**
- **Anxiety.**
- **Past wounds.**

Most people run at this point.

But not you.

You're about to learn how to turn emotional discomfort into emotional strength. And once you do? **You become unshakable.**

* * *

Why Emotional Strength Is Built in Solitude

Think of your emotions like a storm.

Most people react to them like a cheap umbrella in the wind—completely at the mercy of whatever comes their way.

But emotionally resilient people? They are the storm.

They don't react. They observe, process, and move forward.

Here's the secret:

This level of emotional mastery is only built in solitude.

Because when you're alone, there's:

- No one to distract you.
- No one to validate you.
- No one to tell you how to react.

It's just you, your mind, and your ability to take control.

* * *

The Science: How Solitude Rewires Your Emotional Brain

Neuroscience confirms that spending intentional time alone strengthens your emotional resilience.

Here's what happens in your brain when you embrace solitude:

- **Your Prefrontal Cortex Strengthens:** This brain region—responsible for emotional regulation and self-control—becomes more active.
- **Your Amygdala Calms Down:** The part of your brain controlling fear and stress responses becomes less reactive.
- **You Develop Emotional Awareness:** You begin noticing patterns in your emotions rather than simply reacting to them.

In short: **Solitude makes you emotionally bulletproof.**

But only if you know how to use it.

* * *

The 3-Step System for Emotional Resilience

Want to build unshakable mental strength?

Follow this process:

1. **Detach from Your Emotions (Become the Observer)**
2. **Process What You Feel Instead of Avoiding It**
3. **Train Your Nervous System to Handle Discomfort**

* * *

STEP 1: Detach from Your Emotions (Become the Observer)

The #1 Mistake: Thinking your emotions define you.

You are not your emotions.

Yet most people say:

- "I am anxious."
- "I am sad."
- "I am angry."

This is wrong.

You are experiencing anxiety.

You are feeling sadness.

You are not these emotions—they are simply passing through.

When you detach from them, they lose their power over you.

Action Step: The next time you feel overwhelmed, instead of saying "I am [emotion]," say:

- "I am experiencing [emotion], and it will pass."

You are the observer—not the emotion.

* * *

STEP 2: Process What You Feel Instead of Avoiding It

Most people run from emotions. **You need to sit with them.**

Here's the hard truth: **You cannot heal what you refuse to feel.**

Emotions don't disappear when you suppress them. They just wait—showing up later as stress, burnout, anxiety, or self-sabotage.

The only way out is through.

Action Step: The "Sit with It" Exercise

1. When a strong emotion arises, sit down in silence. No phone. No distractions.
2. Name the emotion. What am I feeling?
3. Find where it lives in your body. Is it in your chest? Stomach? Shoulders?
4. Breathe into it. Instead of resisting, allow yourself to feel it fully.

At first, it will be uncomfortable. Then it will lose its grip.

Because when you stop running from emotions, they stop chasing you.

* * *

STEP 3: Train Your Nervous System to Handle Discomfort

Emotional resilience isn't just mental—it's physical.

When you experience stress, fear, or anger, your nervous system reacts:

- Your heart rate spikes.
- Your breathing gets shallow.
- Your body tightens.

If you don't train yourself to handle it, you become controlled by it.

How to Hack Your Nervous System for Emotional Strength:

- **Cold Showers:** Teaches your body to stay calm in discomfort.
- **Deep Breathing:** Slows your heart rate and stops overreaction.
- **Meditation in Silence:** Trains your mind to observe thoughts instead of reacting.

Action Step: The next time you feel overwhelmed, try this:

1. Inhale for 4 seconds.
2. Hold for 4 seconds.
3. Exhale slowly for 8 seconds.

This instantly tells your nervous system: "I am safe."

* * *

Final Thoughts: You Are Stronger Than You Think

The only reason emotions control people is because they never learned how to control them.

Now, you have the tools.

- **You are not your emotions.**
- **You are not your past reactions.**
- **You are not weak.**

You are in control.

Most people will never master emotional resilience. **But you just did.**

* * *

06

Mastering Self-Discipline in Solitude

"Discipline is choosing between what you want now and what you want most."

– Abraham Lincoln

* * *

The Biggest Lie About Self-Discipline

You've been told discipline is about forcing yourself to do things you hate.

Wrong.

Self-discipline isn't about suffering. It's about creating systems that make the right choices effortless.

Think about it:

- If your environment removes distractions, you don't need willpower.
- If your habits align with your goals, you don't need motivation.
- If your routines are designed for focus, you don't need to "push through."

And where do you master this effortless discipline?

In solitude.

When you strip away distractions, all that's left is you and your own mind. The way you train that mind in silence is what shapes your discipline—and, ultimately, your life.

* * *

Why Solitude Is the Ultimate Discipline Hack

Most people never master discipline because they're constantly distracted.

They don't have time to reflect on their habits.

They don't question their daily routines.

They don't stop long enough to identify what's holding them back.

When you embrace solitude:

- **You become brutally self-aware.** No more lying to yourself.
- **You pinpoint exactly where you waste time.** And you know how to cut it out.
- **You create the mental space for change.** Instead of running on autopilot.

In solitude, self-discipline stops being a grind—it becomes the default.

* * *

The 3-Step Framework for Unshakable Discipline

Discipline isn't about willpower. It's about systems.

Follow this process:

1. **Rewire Your Brain for Focus & Control**
2. **Design an Environment That Eliminates Weakness**
3. **Master the Art of Habit Automation**

* * *

STEP 1: Rewire Your Brain for Focus & Control

The Dopamine Detox Method

Your brain is hooked on instant gratification.

Social media, junk food, binge-watching—every time you indulge, your brain gets a dopamine hit.

And here's the catch: dopamine drives motivation.

If you keep rewarding your brain with quick fixes, you'll never stay focused on long-term goals.

The Fix? A dopamine detox.

Action Step: Spend 24 hours without any instant gratification triggers:

- No social media.
- No junk food.
- No passive entertainment.

Replace them with solitude, deep work, or creative tasks. At first, it feels strange. But soon, your brain resets. Focus returns. Discipline gets easier.

* * *

The "Mindful Resistance" Exercise

Most people give up on discipline because they resist discomfort.

New Rule: Sit with discomfort instead of reacting to it.

When you feel an urge (to procrastinate, check your phone, or eat something unhealthy), don't fight it—observe it.

Ask yourself:

- Where do I feel this urge in my body?
- What happens if I just sit with it for 30 seconds?

You'll notice something surprising: the urge fades.

Discipline isn't about fighting impulses. It's about watching them until they lose their grip.

* * *

STEP 2: Design an Environment That Eliminates Weakness

Discipline isn't just mental—it's physical.

The "Make It Impossible" Rule

- If social media distracts you, delete the apps.
- If you waste hours on TV, unplug it after each use.
- If home isn't conducive to focus, find a quieter workspace.

Action Step: Identify one bad habit you want to eliminate and change your environment so it's harder to slip into.

* * *

The Solitude Reset: 60 Minutes of Deep Work Daily

Elite discipline starts with training your brain to focus.

Action Step: Spend one hour every day in solitude, focused on a single task.

- No phone.
- No background music.
- No multitasking.

At first, it's hard. But over time, your focus sharpens. This is how high performers achieve in one hour what most people struggle to accomplish all day.

* * *

STEP 3: Master the Art of Habit Automation

The "Identity Shift" Hack

Most people rely on motivation. That's why they fail.

Example:

- "I should work out." (Motivation-based, easy to quit.)
- "I am the kind of person who never skips a workout." (Identity-based, automatic.)

Action Step: Rewrite your self-talk. Say:

- "I am disciplined."
- "I am someone who takes action."

When you align your identity with your habits, discipline becomes second nature.

* * *

The 2-Minute Habit Rule

Discipline doesn't have to be complicated.

The Rule: Start small—so small it's impossible to fail.

Examples:

- Want to meditate? Start with 2 minutes.
- Want to write? Type one sentence.
- Want to exercise? Do one push-up.

Momentum is everything. Once you start, it's easier to keep going.

Action Step: Pick one new habit and scale it down to 2 minutes.

* * *

Final Thoughts: Discipline is Freedom

Most people think discipline is restrictive.

The truth? **Discipline is freedom.**

Discipline means you control your time.

Discipline means you choose your actions.

Discipline means you build the life you actually want.

And the key to mastering it?

Solitude.

When you remove distractions, face yourself, and design habits with intention, discipline becomes effortless.

* * *

07

Deep Work & Peak Productivity

"The ability to concentrate intensely is a skill that must be trained."

– Cal Newport

* * *

Why Most People Can't Focus (And How You'll Be Different)

Let's be honest.

Most people can't focus for more than 10 minutes. They start a task, get distracted, then spend half an hour scrolling through social media. They confuse "busy" with productive, burning through hours on shallow tasks that don't move the needle.

And here's the truth:

It's not entirely their fault.

The modern world is designed to keep you distracted.

- Your phone is engineered to steal your attention.
- Your inbox constantly pulls you into other people's priorities.
- Your brain, rewired by dopamine hits, craves novelty over depth.

But here's the good news:

Focus is a superpower. And if you master it, you'll outpace everyone.

High achievers—the innovators, top creators, and successful entrepreneurs—all have one thing in common:

They know how to enter deep work mode.

And the secret ingredient?

Solitude.

When you remove distractions and train your mind for deep focus, your productivity and creativity skyrocket.

* * *

What Is Deep Work? (And Why It Changes Everything)

In his book *Deep Work*, Cal Newport defines deep work as:

"The ability to focus without distraction on a cognitively demanding task."

Deep work is the opposite of shallow work:

- **Shallow work:** Constant interruptions, multitasking, surface-level tasks.
- **Deep work:** High concentration, problem-solving, and flow.

It's how:

- **Einstein** developed the theory of relativity.
- **Bill Gates** built Microsoft by taking "Think Weeks" in a secluded cabin.
- **Elon Musk** manages multiple companies by working in focused blocks.

The formula is simple:

Deep work = High productivity + High creativity.

* * *

The Neuroscience of Deep Work: How Solitude Rewires Your Brain

Your brain has two modes:

1. **Focus Mode (Deep Work):** High engagement, problem-solving, creativity.
2. **Scattered Mode (Shallow Work):** Low engagement, constant switching, distraction.

Most people spend their days in scattered mode, chasing quick dopamine hits from notifications, messages, and endless task switching.

Stanford Study: Researchers found that multitasking reduces cognitive efficiency by up to 40%.

The fix? **Structured solitude.**

When you embrace solitude, you train your brain to sustain focus. Over time, distractions lose their grip, and deep work becomes second nature.

* * *

The 4-Step Deep Work System

Want to work like a top performer? Use this framework:

1. **Eliminate Distractions Ruthlessly**
2. **Train Your Brain for Focus**
3. **Use Time Blocks for Maximum Output**
4. **Design a Deep Work Ritual**

* * *

STEP 1: Eliminate Distractions Ruthlessly

The 80/20 Focus Rule

80% of results come from 20% of efforts.

Action Step:

Identify the top 20% of tasks that truly drive your goals. Cut or delegate the rest.

The "No-Notification" Rule

You cannot enter deep work mode if your phone keeps buzzing.

Action Step:

- Turn off all notifications before starting deep work.
- Put your phone in another room.
- Block distracting websites.

Make distraction-free focus your default setting.

* * *

STEP 2: Train Your Brain for Focus

The Focus Sprint Method

Your brain thrives in intense, distraction-free sprints.

Action Step:

1. Set a timer for 50 minutes.
2. Work on one task—no switching.
3. Take a 10-minute break to reset.
4. Repeat.

Do this 3–4 times daily. You'll be amazed at how much you can get done.

The Flow State Trigger

Want to hit peak focus effortlessly?

Use these triggers:

- **Start with a clear goal.** Know exactly what you need to accomplish.

- **Remove all distractions.** Silence your phone, close your tabs, shut the door.
- **Follow a ritual.** (More on that below.)

Within 15–20 minutes, your brain will lock into flow.

* * *

STEP 3: Use Time Blocks for Maximum Output

Deep work isn't about working more hours—it's about working smarter.

Action Step:

Divide your day into focused blocks:

- **Morning Block (2–3 hours):** Use your highest-energy time for your most challenging tasks.
- **Afternoon Block (90 minutes):** Dive into more deep work while energy remains.
- **Evening Block (optional):** Tackle creative tasks, plan for tomorrow, reflect on progress.

Rule: Treat these blocks as sacred. No interruptions.

* * *

STEP 4: Design a Deep Work Ritual

Elite thinkers don't just rely on willpower—they use rituals to trigger deep focus.

Create Your Deep Work Ritual:

- **Pick the same workspace.** Train your brain to associate that place with focus.
- **Use a specific trigger.** A deep breath, a cup of coffee, or a special playlist.
- **Clear all distractions.** Phone off, workspace tidy, notifications silenced.

- **Define a clear goal.** Know exactly what you're working on and why it matters.

Within minutes, your mind will know: *It's time to focus.*

* * *

Final Thoughts: Work Less, Achieve More

Most people waste hours on shallow tasks and distractions. The elite performers know the truth:

Deep work = More results in less time.

Solitude is the gateway to peak productivity.

If you commit to this system for 30 days, you'll be blown away by how much you can accomplish.

Now the question is:

Will you start today?

* * *

08

Visualization – Programming Your Mind for Success

"Whatever the mind can conceive and believe, it can achieve."

– **Napoleon Hill**

* * *

What If Your Brain Could Be Programmed for Success?

What if I told you your brain doesn't know the difference between imagination and reality?

Sounds crazy, right? But science backs it up.

- **Harvard Study:** People who mentally rehearsed piano practice showed the same neural growth as those who physically practiced.
- **Olympic Athletes:** Studies reveal that visualizing a race triggers the same brain circuits as actually running it.
- **Brain Science:** Your Reticular Activating System (RAS) filters what you focus on, making your thoughts shape your reality.

In short: What you visualize, you magnetize.

This is why:

- Elite athletes win championships.
- CEOs build billion-dollar companies.
- Artists bring their visions to life.

And now, so will you.

* * *

Why Visualization Works: The Neuroscience Behind It

Your brain runs on patterns. Every thought and behavior creates a neural pathway.

This is why:

- **Expect failure?** Your brain makes it more likely.
- **Replay mistakes?** They feel real again.
- **Visualize success?** Your brain aligns actions to make it happen.

The Reticular Activating System (RAS): Your Brain's Filter for Reality

Your RAS decides what's important. It's why you hear your name in a noisy room—it's been programmed to notice it.

The secret: Train your RAS to filter for success.

Visualize problems? You find more problems.

Visualize opportunities? Your brain starts spotting them everywhere.

* * *

The 3-Step Visualization Formula

Want to reprogram your mind for success? Follow this system:

1. **See It Clearly:** Create a vivid, detailed mental image of your goal.
2. **Feel It Emotionally:** Engage your senses and emotions to make it feel real.
3. **Act As If:** Align your daily actions with your vision.

* * *

STEP 1: See It Clearly (Mental Rehearsal)

Your brain needs details.

A vague goal won't work. You need a crystal-clear picture.

Action Step: Close your eyes and imagine your goal as if it's happening now.

- What does it look like?
- Where are you? Who's with you?
- What are you doing?

The more vivid, the stronger the effect.

* * *

STEP 2: Feel It Emotionally (Activate the Subconscious)

Here's the key: Emotions make visualization stick.

If you just think about success, nothing changes. But if you feel the pride, excitement, and relief as if it's real, your brain starts believing it.

Action Step: As you visualize, engage those emotions.

- Feel the excitement of reaching your goal.
- Feel the pride of succeeding.
- Feel the freedom you've created.

* * *

STEP 3: Act As If (Align Behavior with Vision)

Visualization isn't wishful thinking—it's a mental workout.

If you believed your vision was real, how would you act today?

- Would you procrastinate?
- Would you make excuses?
- Or would you operate at the level of your future self?

Action Step: Ask yourself each morning:

"What would my future self-do today?"

Then do that.

* * *

Real-World Examples of Visualization in Action

Michael Phelps: Winning Before Swimming

The Olympic swimmer visualized every stroke, turn, and victory long before he hit the water. By race day, his brain was already programmed for gold—resulting in 23 Olympic titles.

Jim Carrey: Manifesting a $10 Million Check

Before his big break, Carrey wrote himself a $10 million check for "acting services rendered." He visualized success, imagined the paychecks, and saw himself as a star. Eventually, he earned that amount for *Dumb and Dumber*.

* * *

Final Thoughts: The Future is Yours to Design

Most people let life happen to them.

The successful ones? **They see it first.**

They visualize it.

They feel it.

They act as if it's already theirs.

This isn't magic. **It's science.**

Your brain is always being programmed.

The question is: **Are you programming it for success?**

Now you have the tools. **Use them.**

* * *

09

Journaling – The Mental Clarity Hack

"We do not write in order to be understood; we write in order to understand."

– C.S. Lewis

* * *

What If Writing Could Rewire Your Brain?

Imagine starting each day by having a raw, honest conversation with your future self.

You ask for guidance.

You reflect on yesterday's lessons.

You chart your next big move.

And then, over time, you notice something odd:

The answers you've been writing? They start becoming real.

The future self you imagined? They were there on the page first.

This isn't fantasy. It's the reason why:

- **Tim Ferriss** calls journaling his "personal therapist."
- **Oprah Winfrey** credits journaling as one of the keys to her success.
- **Richard Branson** writes that every major business move he's ever made started as a journal entry.

Journaling isn't just reflection—it's a thinking tool. A mental blueprint for clarity, strategy, and action.

* * *

Why Most People Journal Wrong (And How You Won't)

Most people approach journaling all wrong.

- **"Dear Diary, today I had a salad."** (Pointless.)
- **"I should write something deep today."** (Forcing insight rarely works.)
- **"I don't know what to say."** (Overthinking kills the process.)

But here's the thing:

Journaling isn't about writing—it's about thinking.

And when done right, it hacks your brain.

- It organizes your thoughts.
- It reduces mental clutter.
- It accelerates decision-making.

Science backs this up:

- **Reduces stress:** Writing about worries calms the brain.
- **Enhances clarity:** Journaling helps you untangle chaotic thoughts.
- **Boosts memory:** The act of writing strengthens cognitive connections.
- **Increases creativity:** Free-flow writing leads to unexpected insights.

In short: Journaling is meditation for people who overthink.

* * *

The 3-Step Journaling System for Clarity & Growth

Follow this framework to journal like the world's top thinkers:

1. **Brain Dump:** Clear mental clutter.
2. **Clarity Prompt:** Ask powerful questions.
3. **Action Journal:** Turn insights into progress.

* * *

STEP 1: Brain Dump – Clear Mental Clutter

Your mind is like a cluttered desk with papers everywhere—thoughts, worries, ideas all fighting for attention.

Journaling clears that desk.

Action Step:

Every morning, set a timer for five minutes. Write down everything swirling in your head.

- No structure.
- No editing.
- Just get it out.

Example Brain Dump:

- "I'm feeling stuck on this project. Maybe I'm overcomplicating it."
- "I keep procrastinating on my workout. Why?"
- "I'm worried about next week's meeting. How can I prepare?"

Result: Your mind feels lighter, your thinking sharper.

* * *

STEP 2: Clarity Prompt – Ask the Right Questions

Your brain is wired to solve problems—but only if you give it the right prompts.

Passive journaling = random thoughts.

Prompt-based journaling = powerful insights.

Action Step:

After your Brain Dump, pick one of these prompts to answer:

- "What's one thing I could do today that would make the biggest difference?"
- "What's holding me back from making progress on X?"
- "What's one small win I can celebrate today?"

Why This Works:

- It shifts your mind from problems to solutions.
- It helps you spot patterns in your thinking and behavior.
- It encourages focused, forward-thinking reflection.

* * *

STEP 3: Action Journal – Bridge Thought to Execution

Journaling that ends on the page is wasted effort. The magic happens when you take action.

Action Step:

End every journaling session with this question:

"What's one small action I can take today based on what I wrote?"

Examples:

- If you're feeling overwhelmed, block out 30 minutes to prioritize your tasks.
- If you're stuck on a decision, write out the pros and cons, then choose one step forward.
- If you've been procrastinating, commit to a 10-minute timer to just start.

Why This Works:

- Journaling isn't about writing—it's about creating momentum.
- The smallest actions lead to bigger wins over time.

* * *

Final Thoughts: Write Your Future into Reality

Every big idea starts as a messy note.

Every breakthrough begins with a curious question.

Every step forward comes from a moment of reflection.

Most people drift through life reacting to whatever comes their way.

But not you.

You've got a tool that:

- Clears mental fog.
- Turns thoughts into actions.
- Makes progress inevitable.

So, what will you write into reality today?

* * *

10

Overcoming Fear & Self-Doubt

"Action cures fear, inaction creates terror."

– Douglas Horton

* * *

The Greatest Enemy You'll Ever Face

Let's cut the fluff—fear is running the show.

It's steering your choices, freezing your ambition, and keeping you in your comfort zone. And it never stops whispering:

- "What if I fail?"
- "What will people think?"
- "I'm not ready yet."

Most people believe these lies.

They cling to "safe" jobs they hate.

They let opportunities slip through their fingers.

They trade their dreams for the illusion of security.

But here's the truth:

Fear isn't real.

It's a mirage—an outdated survival glitch designed to keep you "safe."

And once you learn how to override it, fear transforms into fuel.

* * *

Why Fear is an Illusion (And How to Break Free)

Neuroscience proves fear is just a chemical reaction—cortisol and adrenaline firing off in response to perceived threats. Back when humans lived in the wild, this was helpful. It stopped us from wandering into lion territory.

Today?

Fear is no longer protecting you—it's paralyzing you.

Your brain triggers the same response whether you're being chased by a bear or just sending an important email. The problem isn't the fear itself—it's that we don't realize it's unnecessary.

The Fix?

Reprogram your response.

* * *

The Fear Mastery System: 3 Steps to Overriding Fear

Want to stop fear in its tracks? Follow this blueprint:

1. **Name It** – Define what you're actually afraid of.
2. **Flip It** – Reframe fear as a growth signal.
3. **Act Anyway** – Move forward before fear tightens its grip.

* * *

STEP 1: Name It – Expose Fear for What It Really Is

Fear feeds on vagueness.

When you leave it undefined, it becomes an overwhelming cloud. But the moment you give it a name, it loses its power.

Action Step:

When fear strikes, ask yourself:

- "What exactly am I afraid of?"

Example:

- "I'm afraid to start my own business." (Vague.)
- "I'm afraid I'll fail and people will judge me." (Specific.)

When you pinpoint the fear, you can start dismantling it.

* * *

STEP 2: Flip It – Reframe Fear as a Growth Signal

Fear and excitement feel identical in your body:

- Racing heart.
- Sweaty palms.
- Heightened awareness.

The difference? The story you tell yourself.

Action Step:

Next time fear creeps in, try this reframe:

- Instead of "I'm scared to fail," say: "I'm excited to grow."
- Instead of "I'm nervous to present," say: "I'm thrilled to share my ideas."

Why It Works:

Reframing fear as excitement tricks your brain into associating it with growth instead of danger.

* * *

STEP 3: Act Anyway – Train Yourself to Move Through Fear

Fear gains power the longer you wait. The fix? Immediate action.

Action Step:

When fear appears:

1. Count down—5, 4, 3, 2, 1.
2. Take the next step.

Examples:

- Afraid to speak up in a meeting? Count down, then raise your hand.
- Afraid to launch a new project? Count down, then take the first step.

Lesson:

Action doesn't just cure fear—it annihilates it.

* * *

Real-World Examples: Fear in Action

Will Smith: Jumping Out of a Plane to Beat Fear

Will Smith once described how the anticipation of skydiving terrified him—until he jumped. The fear wasn't real; it existed only before the action. Once he leaped, the fear vanished.

Michael Jordan: Using Failure as Fuel

Jordan missed thousands of shots, lost hundreds of games, and failed repeatedly. But he never let fear stop him from taking the next shot. That's why he's the GOAT.

* * *

Final Thoughts: Fear Will Not Control You

Here's the hard truth:

Fear never really goes away.

But you can stop it from ruling your life.

- Fear is normal—but letting it control you is a choice.
- Fear doesn't mean stop—it means move.
- The life you want exists just past the discomfort of fear.

You don't need more time. You need more courage.

And now? You've got it.

* * *

11

Decision-Making & Intuition

"You have to trust in something—your gut, destiny, life, karma, whatever."

– Steve Jobs

* * *

Why Most People Struggle with Decisions

Let's be real.

Most people overthink decisions until they freeze.

- They ask everyone they know for advice.
- They analyze every possible outcome.
- They hesitate, delay, and then end up doing nothing.

The result? Constant second-guessing and zero momentum.

Meanwhile, high achievers trust their instincts, commit to their choices, and move forward without looking back.

The difference? They trust their intuition.

And after this chapter, so will you.

* * *

The Myth of "Right" and "Wrong" Decisions

The belief that every decision has a clear "right" or "wrong" answer keeps most people stuck.

But here's the truth:

- **Every decision gives you either the result you want or the lesson you need.**
- **There's no failure—just data.**
- **Action moves you forward. Indecision keeps you stuck.**

Reframe it: Instead of asking, "What if this is wrong?" ask,

"What can I learn from this?"

* * *

The Science of Intuition: How Your Brain Makes Smart Decisions Instantly

Intuition is just fast, subconscious decision-making.

Here's what's happening in your brain:

- Your mind is constantly processing patterns, experiences, and subtle cues.
- The more you experience, the faster your brain identifies what works and what doesn't.
- That "gut feeling" is simply your brain giving you an answer before your conscious mind can.

Example: Ever meet someone and feel something was "off"? That's your brain recognizing subtle, familiar patterns before you can articulate them.

The catch?

Most people ignore their intuition because they've been taught to overthink everything.

Not anymore.

* * *

The Intuitive Decision-Making Framework (3 Steps to Making Bold Choices)

If you want to make fast, confident decisions, follow this framework:

1. **Silence the Noise – Give Yourself Space to Think**
2. **Make a Fast, Confident Choice – The 80% Rule**
3. **Commit & Adjust – Build Trust in Your Gut**

* * *

STEP 1: Silence the Noise – Give Yourself Space to Think

The Problem: Most people drown out their own intuition.

- They ask for too many opinions.
- They let fear overshadow their instincts.
- They never give themselves quiet time to listen to their gut.

The Fix: Solitude.

Action Step: Solo Clarity Session

1. Find a quiet spot. No phone, no distractions.
2. Take 5 deep breaths. Clear your head.
3. Ask yourself: **"If I already knew the answer, what would it be?"**
4. Write down your first instinct.

Why It Works:

When you eliminate noise, your intuition has a chance to speak.

* * *

STEP 2: Make a Fast, Confident Choice – The 80% Rule

The Mistake: Most people wait for 100% certainty before deciding.

But here's the thing: **100% certainty never comes.**

The 80% Rule: If you're at least 80% sure, make the call.

Action Step:

When you're faced with a decision, ask yourself: **"Am I at least 80% sure about this?"**

If the answer is yes, decide now.

* * *

STEP 3: Commit & Adjust – Build Trust in Your Gut

The Mistake: Doubting your own decisions.

The Fix: Commit, move forward, and adapt as needed.

Action Step: The No Looking Back Rule

Once you make a choice:

- **Stop analyzing.**
- **Stop second-guessing.**
- Move forward. Adjust, if necessary, later, but don't hesitate now.

Lesson: Success isn't about perfect decisions. Its about bold decisions followed by quick adjustments.

* * *

Real-World Examples: Intuition in Action

Elon Musk: Making Big Bets Without Hesitation

Musk risks everything when his gut tells him it's right.

- He bet Tesla on an unproven electric market.
- He doubled down on SpaceX when everyone doubted him.

Lesson: Bold decisions lead to bold results.

Oprah Winfrey: Trusting Her Inner Voice

Oprah's secret? She follows her gut.

- She turned down deals that didn't "feel right."
- She built her empire by listening to that quiet inner voice.

Lesson: The more you listen to your intuition, the sharper it becomes.

* * *

Final Thoughts: The Era of Indecision is Over

Here's the truth:

- You already have the answers inside you.
- Your intuition is smarter than your overthinking.
- Fast decisions = fast progress.

The next time you hesitate, remember:

- You don't need more opinions.
- You don't need perfect clarity.
- You need to trust yourself and move.

It's time to decide.

* * *

12

The Power of Creative Solitude

"Silence is the speech of the awakened."

– Swami Vivekananda

* * *

Where Do Breakthrough Ideas Really Come From?

Let's clear up a myth.

People assume great ideas are born in group discussions, brainstorming sessions, and think tanks.

Sure, collaboration can refine ideas, but the spark of true innovation?

It starts in solitude.

History proves it:

- **Sage Vyasa** meditated in silence before composing the Mahabharata.
- **Leonardo da Vinci** retreated to study nature and sketch inventions far ahead of his time.
- **Nikola Tesla** visualized entire machines alone before ever building them.

But they didn't stop there.

After finding clarity in solitude, they returned to share, test, and refine their ideas with others.

The truth is:

- Solitude is where ideas are born.
- Collaboration is where ideas evolve.

In our hyper-connected world, most people skip the first step—solitude.

This chapter will show you how to reclaim it and harness its power.

* * *

Why Solitude Fuels Creativity: The Ancient & Scientific Perspective

The Ancient View: Wisdom from Hinduism & Zen

Ancient traditions have long understood the power of silence:

- **Hindu Upanishads**: The mind is like a lake. When disturbed, it can't reflect clearly. When still, it reveals truth.
- **Zen Buddhism**: Through "Wu Wei" (effortless action), insights arise naturally when the mind is at rest.
- **Yogic Tradition**: Mauna, the practice of silence, sharpens the intellect and opens the door to higher thinking.

The Scientific View: How the Brain Works in Solitude

Neuroscience backs up what sages knew:

Your brain operates in two modes:

1. **Surface Thinking Mode** (constant input): Processes information but struggles with deep insights.
2. **Deep Processing Mode** (solitude): Finds unexpected connections, generating fresh, creative breakthroughs.

Key Point:

- Great ideas don't come from overthinking. They emerge when you stop.

* * *

The 3-Step Creative Solitude Framework

Want to unlock original ideas and deep insights? Follow this system:

1.   **Empty – Clear Your Mental Clutter**
2.   **Absorb – Enter the Creative Field**
3.   **Manifest – Turn Ideas into Reality**

* * *

STEP 1: Empty – Clear Your Mental Clutter

Creativity's biggest enemy? Overload.

Most people never stop consuming:

- Endless scrolling.
- Nonstop podcasts.
- Constant social media updates.

The result?

Your mind becomes a chaotic inbox—too full to find clarity.

Action Step: The 24-Hour Creative Fast

For one day, eliminate all non-essential input:

- No social media.
- No news.
- No passive entertainment.

Instead, sit alone with your thoughts.

It will feel uncomfortable at first. Then clarity will emerge.

Why This Works:

Hindu sages called this Mauna Vrata—a vow of silence that helps you declutter your mind and access deeper thought.

* * *

STEP 2: Absorb – Enter the Creative Field

Where do ideas really come from?

- **Hinduism:** Creativity flows from Brahman (universal consciousness).
- **Zen Buddhism:** Insights emerge when the ego is silent and the mind is present.
- **Modern Neuroscience:** Creativity happens when your subconscious mind connects patterns outside of logical thinking.

The common thread:

Stop forcing ideas. Start allowing them.

Action Step: The Deep Listening Method

1. Find a quiet, distraction-free place.
2. Sit in silence for 20 minutes.
3. Pay attention to thoughts, images, and feelings that arise.

Why This Works:

The moment you stop trying to create is the moment your best ideas appear.

* * *

STEP 3: Manifest – Turn Ideas into Reality

Creativity is useless if it stays in your head.

The great creators—Tesla, da Vinci, Edison—didn't just imagine their ideas; they brought them to life.

Action Step: The Visualization-to-Action Technique

1. Close your eyes and vividly imagine your idea as if it's already real.
2. Write down the idea in detail—make it tangible.
3. Take one immediate action toward it.

Why This Works:

- In Yogic terms, this is Sankalpa—intention turned into action.
- The act of writing and taking that first step sets the creative process in motion.

* * *

Final Thoughts: The Silence That Unlocks Greatness

Most people try to force creativity. They chase it through nonstop input, brainstorming marathons, and frantic problem-solving.

You know better.

- Creativity begins in silence.
- It thrives in the space where you can think, reflect, and dream.
- And it becomes real only when you act on it.

The path is clear.

Step into solitude—and create.

* * *

13

The Partner Paradox & Relationship Mastery

"The quality of your life is determined by the quality of your relationships."

– Tony Robbins

* * *

The Relationship Paradox: Why Being Alone Makes You Better at Love

Most people think the secret to a strong relationship is constant togetherness.

Never apart. Never alone. Always connected.

But here's the paradox:

The best relationships are built by people who are comfortable being alone.

- If you don't know who you are without someone else, you become dependent.
- If you rely on a partner to "complete" you, you put unbearable pressure on the relationship.
- If you lose yourself in the connection, the connection ultimately weakens.

Psychology Insight: Research shows that interdependent relationships—where both partners maintain individuality—lead to greater happiness and long-term success.

The healthiest relationships aren't about needing someone. They're about choosing them.

* * *

How Your Attachment Style Shapes Your Relationships

Your attachment style, developed in childhood, deeply affects how you approach love, intimacy, and trust as an adult.

The Four Attachment Styles (Which One Are You?)

1. **Secure Attachment (The Relationship Masters)**

    o   Comfortable with closeness and independence.
    o   Communicates openly, handles conflict with trust.
    o   Result: Stable, loving relationships.

2. **Anxious Attachment (The Overthinkers)**

    o   Craves closeness, fears abandonment.
    o   Overanalyzes every interaction, seeks constant reassurance.
    o   Result: Feeling insecure, always chasing love.

3. **Avoidant Attachment (The Lone Wolves)**

    o   Fears intimacy, values independence over closeness.
    o   Struggles to open up emotionally.
    o   Result: Avoids deep connection, stays distant.

4. **Fearful-Avoidant (The Push-Pull Cycle)**

    o   Desires closeness but fears being hurt.
    o   Hot-and-cold behavior—loving one moment, distant the next.
    o   Result: Self-sabotage, unstable relationships.

* * *

How to Rewire Your Attachment Style

The good news:

Attachment styles are not permanent. You can change them.

Action Steps:

- If you're anxious, practice self-soothing instead of seeking external validation.
- If you're avoidant, work on opening up and being vulnerable.
- If you're fearful-avoidant, focus on building emotional stability before diving into deep intimacy.

The goal: Develop a secure attachment—where love is a choice, not a need.

* * *

The 3-Part Relationship Mastery Framework

Ready to build a strong, fulfilling relationship? Follow this blueprint:

1. **Master Yourself Before Seeking Love**
2. **Build Interdependence, Not Codependence**
3. **Communicate Like a Relationship Expert**

* * *

STEP 1: Master Yourself Before Seeking Love

The #1 Relationship Mistake: Thinking someone else will "complete" you.

Reality Check:

- A relationship can't fill the void of a weak self-identity.
- Love doesn't fix you—it enhances who you already are.

Action Step:

Before starting or improving a relationship, ask:

- "Who am I outside of this relationship?"
- "If this relationship ended, would I still feel whole?"

When you feel complete on your own, you bring your best self into the partnership.

* * *

STEP 2: Build Interdependence, Not Codependence

The Secret: Balance intimacy with independence.

Codependence:

- "I can't be happy without you."
- Relationships feel suffocating and dependent.

Interdependence:

- "I love you, but I'm whole on my own."
- Relationships feel supportive and empowering.

Action Step: The Together Alone Practice

1. Spend intentional time apart. Develop hobbies, passions, and individual goals.
2. Support your partner's growth without feeling threatened.
3. Reunite as two strong individuals, creating a dynamic, exciting connection.

* * *

STEP 3: Communicate Like a Relationship Expert

Fact: The #1 predictor of relationship success is how couples handle conflict.

Toxic patterns to avoid:

- Blaming and criticizing.
- Stonewalling (shutting down emotionally).
- Reacting emotionally instead of responding with clarity.

Action Step: The Pause & Respond Technique

1. When conflict arises, pause before reacting.
2. Take three deep breaths and ask: "Am I reacting from emotion or logic?"
3. Speak with curiosity instead of blame.

Why It Works:

Strong relationships aren't conflict-free—they're conflict-resilient.

* * *

Final Thoughts: Love is a Skill, Not Just an Emotion

The truth:

- Great relationships aren't built by luck—they're built by design.
- Love thrives when both partners are whole individuals.
- Independence and self-awareness create the foundation for deep, lasting connection.

The question is:

Are you bringing your best self into your relationships?

Because once you do, love becomes effortless.

* * *

14

The Art of Letting Go

"You can't start the next chapter of your life if you keep re-reading the last one."

– Unknown

* * *

Why Letting Go Feels Impossible (But isn't)

Let's be honest.

You know you should let go.

You know the past is over.

You know holding on hurts you more than anyone else.

And yet...

- You still replay old memories.
- You still cling to relationships that ended long ago.
- You still carry beliefs about yourself that no longer fit.

Why?

Because your brain is wired for attachment.

Even when something is toxic or outdated, your mind resists change.

Even when you know better, your emotions lag behind.

Letting go isn't just a decision—it's a mental retraining process.

The good news?

You can rewire your mind to release, reset, and move forward.

This chapter will show you how.

* * *

Why Your Brain Holds On (The Psychology of Attachment)

Psychologists have found that three common mental traps keep us stuck in the past:

1. The "Endowment Effect" – Overvaluing What You Have

Your brain hates losing things. Studies show people cling to something—even if it's worthless—just because they own it.

This applies to relationships, jobs, and even pain. You don't hold on because it's good. You hold on because it's familiar.

Solution: Reframe the loss as a gain.

Action Step: Ask yourself: **"What am I gaining by letting go?"**

- Peace of mind?
- Emotional freedom?
- Space for new opportunities?

When your brain sees letting go as a win, it becomes easier.

* * *

2. The "Narrative Trap" – Getting Stuck in Your Story

We attach to stories, even painful ones:

- "I was betrayed, so I can't trust anyone."
- "I failed once, so I'm destined to fail."
- "If I let this go, I lose part of myself."

Reality Check: These are just stories. You can rewrite them.

Action Step: Try the **Narrative Rewrite Exercise:**

1. Write down the story you've been telling yourself.
2. Challenge it: **"Is this fact, or just a belief?"**
3. Rewrite it into something empowering.

Example: Instead of:

"I was betrayed, so I can't trust again," try:

"I've learned what I deserve, and now I trust myself to choose better."

* * *

3. The "Emotional Residue Effect" – Your Brain is Addicted to the Past

Strong emotions create deep neural pathways.

This is why heartbreak, rejection, and loss feel so intense.

Your brain replays the past in an attempt to protect you from future pain.

Solution: Release the emotion, not just the thought.

Action Step: Use the **Emotional Release Method:**

1. **Feel it fully:** Stop suppressing. Sit with the emotion for 90 seconds.
2. **Label it:** "I feel anger" or "I feel grief." Naming it reduces its power.
3. **Physically release it:** Write, run, or scream into a pillow—get it out of your system.

Letting go is not just mental—it's physical. You must move the energy out.

* * *

The 3-Step Letting Go Framework

Here's a simple system:

1. **Accept – Stop Fighting Reality**
2. **Detach – Break the Emotional Loop**
3. **Redirect – Focus on Your Future**

* * *

STEP 1: Accept – Stop Fighting Reality

The Mistake: Denial.

- "This shouldn't have happened."
- "It's not fair."
- "I wish I could change it."

Reality Check: It happened.

Wishing it were different only keeps you stuck.

Fighting reality creates suffering.

Action Step: Use the **Radical Acceptance Exercise:**

1. Say out loud: **"This happened. I can't change it. I accept this reality."**
2. Feel the discomfort—and notice how it begins to lose its grip.

Reminder: Acceptance doesn't mean approval. It means peace over resistance.

* * *

STEP 2: Detach – Break the Emotional Loop

Your brain treats thoughts like reality. If you keep replaying painful memories, you reinforce their power.

Solution: Disrupt the loop.

Action Step: Try the **Thought Disruptor Technique:**

1. When a painful memory surfaces, label it as "not useful."
2. Redirect your focus to something neutral or positive.

Result: By breaking the cycle, you weaken the memory's grip.

* * *

STEP 3: Redirect – Focus on Your Future

The Mistake: Trying to "let go" without filling the void.

The Fix: Shift your focus forward.

Action Step: Try the **Future Focus Rewire:**

1. Set a new goal or challenge—something exciting.
2. Surround yourself with new experiences and positive influences.
3. Create a vision bigger than your past.

When your brain has a new target, it stops clinging to the old.

* * *

Final Thoughts: The Freedom of Letting Go

Here's the truth:

- Letting go isn't about forgetting—it's about freeing yourself.
- Your past has no power unless you keep feeding it.
- The moment you shift your focus forward, the weight lifts.

Are you ready to let go?

Because once you do, you'll create space for something better.

* * *

15

Mastering the Inner Critic

"It's not who you are that holds you back, it's who you think you're not."

— Denis Waitley

* * *

The Voice in Your Head is Lying to You

Let's be honest:

- You've doubted yourself.
- You've told yourself you're not good enough.
- You've hesitated because that voice in your head said, "What if you fail?"

That voice?

It's your Inner Critic. And it's been running the show for years.

But here's the truth:

- Your Inner Critic is not a truth-teller.
- It's a survival mechanism that keeps you stuck in fear.

Psychology shows that self-doubt is learned—shaped by childhood experiences, societal expectations, and past failures.

And here's the best part: If it's learned, it can be unlearned.

* * *

Why Your Brain Creates an Inner Critic (The Science of Self-Doubt)

Neuroscientists have identified three mental patterns that feed your Inner Critic:

1. The "Negativity Bias"

- **What it is:** Your brain over-focuses on failures, not successes.
- **Why it happens:** It's a survival instinct. Your mind remembers pain to avoid it in the future.
- **How it affects you:** Even if you succeed once but fail twice, your brain fixates on the failures.
- **Solution:** Retrain your brain to notice wins.

Action Step:

- Write down 5 small victories from your life.
- Review them every time self-doubt sneaks in.

* * *

2. The "Comparison Trap"

- **What it is:** Comparing your real life to other people's highlight reels.
- **Why it happens:** social media amplifies perfection, making you feel like you're always falling behind.
- **How it affects you:** You judge yourself against an incomplete picture, fueling self-doubt.
- **Solution:** Reframe comparisons to gain perspective.

Action Step:

- When you compare yourself to someone, ask:
    - "Do I have the full picture of their struggles?"
    - "Would I trade my entire life for theirs?"
- Answer honestly—and most often, it's a no.

* * *

3. The "Imposter Syndrome Loop"

- **What it is:** Feeling like a fraud, even when you succeed.
- **Why it happens:** The more you achieve, the more your Inner Critic tries to pull you back.
- **How it affects you:** It keeps you in your comfort zone and makes you second-guess your accomplishments.
- **Solution:** Reframe discomfort as growth.

Action Step:

- Next time you feel like an imposter, remind yourself:

    o "If I feel uncomfortable, it means I'm leveling up."

- Use fear as a signal that you're expanding.

* * *

The 3-Step Inner Critic Mastery Framework

Ready to take back control? Follow these steps:

1. **Identify – Catch the Inner Critic in Action**
2. **Reframe – Challenge & Rewire Negative Thoughts**
3. **Replace – Build a Confident Inner Voice**

* * *

STEP 1: Identify – Catch the Inner Critic in Action

The problem: Negative thoughts often run on autopilot, so you don't even notice them.

The fix: Bring them into the light.

Action Step:

- For one day, write down every self-doubting thought that crosses your mind.

- Example:

  - "I'm not smart enough to do this."
  - "I always mess things up."

Why it works: Awareness is the first step to change.

* * *

STEP 2: Reframe – Challenge & Rewire Negative Thoughts

The problem: Your brain strengthens whatever you repeat—so negative self-talk becomes ingrained.

The fix: Challenge it and create new mental pathways.

Action Step:

- Take a negative thought and ask:

  - "Is this 100% true?"
  - "Would I say this to a friend?"
  - "What's a more empowering way to see this?"

- Example:

  - From "I'm terrible at public speaking" → "I'm improving every time I speak."

Why it works: Thoughts are not facts. When you reframe them, you take back control.

* * *

STEP 3: Replace – Build a Confident Inner Voice

The problem: Positive self-talk feels fake if it's not backed by evidence.

The fix: Pair it with action.

Action Step:

- Each night, write down one small win from your day.

- Say out loud:

    o "I am someone who takes action."
    o "I am capable and improving every day."

Why it works: Confidence is built one small win at a time.

* * *

Final Thoughts: Your Inner Critic is Not the Boss

- **Truth:** Your Inner Critic will always be there, but it doesn't have to run your life.
- **Reality:** Self-doubt is just an old habit. You can break it.
- **Empowerment:** Confidence isn't something you're born with— it's something you build.

So here's the question:

Are you ready to silence the self-doubt and own your full potential?

Because once you do? **Nothing can stop you.**

* * *

16

Reprogramming Limiting Beliefs

"Whether you think you can or think you can't, you're right."

– Henry Ford

* * *

What If Everything Holding You Back Is Just a Lie?

Picture this.

What if the only reason you haven't reached your full potential is because of what you believe?

What if the boundaries you see all around you are just shadows in your mind?

The truth?

Your beliefs shape your reality.

If you believe success is hard, you'll make it hard.

If you believe wealth is scarce, you'll block opportunities without even realizing it.

If you believe you're not good enough, you won't take the risks that lead to greatness.

Your brain doesn't work to uncover the truth. It works to confirm whatever you already believe.

The good news?

Change your beliefs, and your world will shift with them.

* * *

Why Your Brain Holds onto Limiting Beliefs

(The Psychology of Conditioning)

Limiting beliefs don't just appear out of nowhere.

They're shaped, wired, and reinforced over time by three key factors:

* * *

1. Childhood Programming *(Your First Mental Operating System)*

Think back. Between the ages of 0 and 7, your brain was a sponge.

You absorbed what your parents, teachers, and society told you—without question.

- **"Money doesn't grow on trees."** → You learn that wealth is hard to come by.
- **"You're not the smart one in the family."** → You doubt your abilities.
- **"Stick to what you know."** → You fear taking risks.

This early programming becomes your default mental operating system.

But like any outdated software, you can update it.

Action Step: The Belief Audit

- Pick one belief that's holding you back.
- Ask: "Where did this belief come from? Is it really mine?"
- If it's not, delete it. You're the programmer now.

* * *

2. The Confirmation Bias Loop *(Your Brain's Reality Filter)*

Your brain is a pro at proving itself right.

If you believe "I'm not a leader," you'll overlook the times you took charge.

If you believe "I always fail," you'll highlight mistakes and ignore wins.

This is called confirmation bias. And it's not a bad thing—if you know how to hack it.

Action Step: The Counter-Evidence Challenge

- Pick a limiting belief.
- Find three examples that prove it wrong.
- Review these daily until your brain gets the message.

When you focus on evidence that challenges the belief, you rewire your mind.

* * *

3. Emotional Anchors *(Pain That Holds You Back)*

Think about a time when you felt rejected, embarrassed, or defeated.

That emotional memory locked in a belief:

- **"I'll never be good enough."**
- **"I'm not lovable."**
- **"I shouldn't even try."**

These strong emotions create deep neural grooves.

But just as they were formed, they can be reshaped.

Action Step: Emotional Release Method

- Recall a painful memory tied to a limiting belief.
- Ask: "What lesson did this teach me that made me stronger?"

- Visualize releasing that memory's hold on you.
- Replace it with an empowering statement.

* * *

Real-World Examples: Belief Breakthroughs

Jim Carrey's $10 Million Check

- Raised in poverty, Jim Carrey once believed that wealth was impossible.
- He wrote himself a $10 million check and carried it around.
- Later, he earned that exact amount for *Dumb and Dumber*.

Lesson: Your mind moves toward the reality you program into it.

* * *

Roger Bannister & The 4-Minute Mile

- Before 1954, everyone "knew" the human body couldn't run a mile in under four minutes.
- Bannister ignored that belief—and smashed the record.
- Within a year, others followed, because the "impossible" was no longer impossible.

Lesson: The limits you accept are the limits you'll live by.

* * *

The 3-Step Belief Reprogramming Framework

Want to rewrite your mental blueprint?

Follow these steps:

* * *

Step 1: Identify the Belief

(Find Your Mental Block)

Start by shining a light on what's holding you back.

Most people don't even know their beliefs are programmed against them.

Action Step: Belief Scan

- Write down your thoughts about:

    o Money → Do you see it as abundant or scarce?
    o Success → Do you believe you deserve it?
    o Love → Do you expect it, or do you fear rejection?

Identify the patterns. Awareness is the first step.

* * *

Step 2: Challenge the Belief

(Break the Mental Loop)

Once you find the belief, question it.

Your brain isn't attached to truth—it's attached to habit.

Action Step: The "What If I'm Wrong?" Method

- Take a belief like: "I can't succeed in business."
- Ask: "What if that's not true? What if I can learn and improve?"
- Find proof that contradicts the belief.

Your mind loves evidence. Feed it better evidence.

* * *

Step 3: Replace the Belief

(Install a New Mindset)

If you want to delete an old program, you need to replace it with a new one.

Repetition is key.

Action Step: The New Identity Technique

- Choose a belief you want to install.

    o Example: "I am a confident, capable leader."

- Repeat it daily:

    o **Morning mantra:** "I am becoming more confident every day."

- Act as if it's already true.

When you consistently think, say, and act according to this belief, it sticks.

* * *

Final Thoughts: You Are Not Your Old Beliefs

What you believe now isn't permanent.

- It was taught to you.
- You can unlearn it.
- You can reprogram it.

When you shift your inner world, your outer world follows.

The question is:

What will you believe about yourself next?

* * *

17

The Power of Identity Shifting

"We don't rise to the level of our goals; we fall to the level of our identity."

– James Clear

* * *

Your Identity is Just a Story You Keep Telling Yourself

Let's flip the script for a moment.

Who do you believe you are?

Are you the labels you've been given—"the quiet one," "the underdog," "the non-athlete"?

Are you the product of your past failures, the person who "never gets it right"?

Or are you something more?

Here's the deal: *You are not fixed.*

Your identity isn't some permanent tattoo etched into your psyche. It's more like a pair of glasses—easily swapped out, but the lenses you choose determine how you see yourself and the world. You act shy because you believe you're shy. You self-sabotage relationships because you think you're "bad at love." You avoid success because, deep down, you think it's for "other people."

Sound familiar?

Psychology Insight: Your brain is wired to cling to a consistent self-image—even if it's negative. This is what psychologists call *self-concept bias*. You'll fight like hell to keep being "you" because it feels safe—even if that "you" is holding you back.

But what if you could swap out those glasses?

What if the story you keep telling yourself is just that—a story?

* * *

Why Your Brain Clings to an Old Identity

Understanding the psychology of self-concept

Your current identity is a well-worn pattern in your brain. Neuroscientists have discovered three key loops that keep you locked into that pattern:

1. The Label Loop (You Become What You Keep Calling Yourself)

Ever heard this growing up:

"You're so shy."
"You'll never be good at math."
"You're not a natural leader."

As a child, you absorbed these labels, often without question. The more you repeated them, the more your brain etched them into your self-concept.

Action Step: The Identity Audit Exercise

- Write down every label you've internalized.
- Cross out the ones that don't serve you.
- Replace them with empowering alternatives.

What you call yourself matters. Your brain listens.

2. The Habit Reinforcement Loop (Behavior Shapes Belief)

People think identity is the cause of behavior. It's not.

It's the result.

You don't become a fit person by deciding you're "fit."

You become fit by exercising consistently.

And over time, your brain shifts: "I'm the kind of person who works out."

Action Step: The Small Wins Identity Shift

Pick one behavior aligned with the identity you want.

- Want to be a writer? Write one sentence each morning.
- Want to be a confident speaker? Speak up once in a meeting. Do this daily. Your brain rewires through repetition.

3. The Social Mirror Loop (You Reflect What Others See)

Humans are social creatures. If you've always been "the quiet one" in your family, you might keep playing that role, even when it no longer fits.

If your coworkers see you as "the spreadsheet guy" instead of the visionary, you might hesitate to step into a leadership role.

Action Step: The Identity Environment Check

- Identify who reinforces your current identity.
- Seek out people who see the version of you that you want to become.
- Your environment reflects your identity. Change the reflection, and your identity starts to shift.

* * *

Real-World Examples of Identity Shifting

Example 1: Muhammad Ali—Declaring Greatness

Before he was "The Greatest," Ali called himself that every chance he got. He told the world who he was before anyone agreed. Over time, his actions caught up with his words, and his identity as a champion became reality.

Lesson: Declare who you want to be. Say it before you see it.

Example 2: Arnold Schwarzenegger—Reinvention on Repeat

Arnold didn't stop at "bodybuilder." He declared himself an actor, then a politician. He adopted the new identity first, then acted accordingly until the world caught up.

Lesson: Identity is fluid. Decide who you are, then let your actions align.

* * *

The 3-Step Identity Shifting Framework

Step 1: Define—Create the Blueprint

- Don't just say, "I want to be more confident."
- Get specific: *"I am someone who speaks up in every meeting, asks for what I want, and carries myself with ease."*
  Write it down. Review it daily. This is your identity blueprint.

Step 2: Align—Act as If

Start acting like the person you want to become. Not tomorrow. Not next year. *Now.*

Even small actions—like raising your hand, taking a tiny risk, or speaking a little louder—reinforce the new identity.

Step 3: Reinforce—Lock it In

Identity isn't a one-time decision. It's a practice.

- Every time you act in alignment with your new identity, write it down.
- Celebrate the wins, no matter how small.
- Over time, your brain catches on: *This is who I am now.*

* * *

Final Thoughts: Who Will You Decide to Be?

You're not your past. You're not your failures. You're not the labels someone else stuck on you.

Your identity is your choice.

And when you change your identity, you change your life.

* * *

18

Breaking Free From Approval Trap

"If you live for people's acceptance, you will die from their rejection."

– Lecrae

* * *

Why Do We Care So Much About What Others Think?

It's a familiar trap.

Have you ever bitten your tongue, hesitated on a bold move, or felt a tightening in your chest all because of that nagging question: "What will people think?" It's not just you—our brains are hardwired this way.

Evolutionary psychology reveals that our ancestors survived by being part of a tribe. Back then, rejection wasn't just embarrassing—it was life-threatening. Today, while rejection might only mean an awkward pause at the dinner table, our brains still treat disapproval like a saber-tooth tiger lurking in the shadows.

But here's the truth: If you let external opinions run the show, you'll never take center stage in your own life. You'll stay in the safe lane, living for others, and missing the magic of being unapologetically you.

It's time to break free.

* * *

The Mental Trap: Why Approval Feels So Good (and So Dangerous)

Think of approval as a sugar rush for the mind.

When someone likes your post or gives you a compliment, your brain fires off a hit of dopamine—the same feel-good chemical that lights up when you win a small prize or eat something sweet. It feels amazing, but it comes with a cost: dependence. Soon, you're chasing validation not because it adds value, but because it's a quick fix. Over time, your internal compass—your own sense of worth—gets drowned out by the noise of others' opinions.

But here's the thing: That rush? It's a lie. It's fleeting. And when it fades, you're left needing another hit, more desperate than before.

This cycle is why so many people never try, never speak out, never dare. It's not because they don't have ideas or ambition—it's because they're hooked on approval, addicted to the validation that keeps them safely in place.

But you're about to cut through that noise.

* * *

Breaking Free: The Confidence to Stand Alone

Imagine this: What if you were perfectly okay with someone disagreeing with you? What if you didn't need every comment to be a thumbs-up or every idea to be universally applauded? The truth is, once you stop needing everyone's approval, you become unstoppable.

You've likely heard that the greatest thinkers, artists, and entrepreneurs didn't wait for permission to create. They didn't look to the crowd for confirmation. Instead, they stood firmly in their vision, even when the world scoffed.

Steve Jobs was called crazy. Oprah was told she'd never make it on TV. J.K. Rowling's manuscript was rejected by multiple publishers. The difference? They knew who they were and what they wanted. Their power didn't come from applause—it came from self-assurance. They weren't chasing approval. They were chasing excellence.

And you can do the same.

* * *

How to Train Your Mind to Value Your Own Voice

Rewiring your brain to break free from the approval trap isn't about suddenly turning into a rebel or ignoring everyone's opinions. It's about shifting the balance. Here's how:

1. **Pause Before You Seek Validation:**
   Before you post that update, send that message, or ask for feedback, pause. Ask yourself, "Am I doing this because I believe in it, or because I'm hoping for praise?"

2. **Focus on Contribution, Not Reaction:**
   Instead of wondering how people will respond, think about what you're bringing to the table. If you believe your idea, art, or work will make a difference, the audience's reaction is secondary. Shift from "Will they like me?" to "How can I help them?"

3. **Embrace Rejection as a Sign of Growth:**
   Rejection isn't a stop sign—it's a stepping stone. The more you put yourself out there, the more rejections you'll get. But here's the kicker: You'll also get more wins, more breakthroughs, and more respect. The key is to see rejection not as proof you're not good enough, but as evidence you're playing a bigger game.

4. **Practice Being Unpopular (Once in a While):**
   Not every choice needs to be a crowd-pleaser. Try making a decision this week that's entirely for you—not for applause, not for agreement, just because it feels right. Notice how liberating it is to trust your own judgment.

* * *

The Shift That Changes Everything

You don't have to wait for approval to start living the life you want. You don't have to check everyone's reaction before making a move. When you stop chasing validation, you gain something much more valuable: freedom.

And that freedom? It's the key to unlocking your full potential.

* * *

19

The Power of Being Disliked

"The only way to avoid criticism is to do nothing, say nothing, and be nothing."

– Aristotle

* * *

Why Do We Fear Being Disliked?

Let's be real.

Have you ever stayed silent instead of speaking your truth because you feared judgment?

Have you ever avoided taking action because you worried what people might say?

Have you ever felt drained trying to be "likable" to everyone?

If so, you're not alone.

Your brain is wired to seek acceptance.

Evolutionarily, being part of a tribe meant survival. Rejection meant danger.

Your brain still reacts to social disapproval as if it's life-threatening (even though it isn't).

This is why criticism stings, disagreement feels personal, and being "left out" triggers anxiety.

But here's the truth: Trying to be liked by everyone is the fastest way to lose yourself.

This chapter will show you how to embrace being disliked, own your authenticity, and become truly fearless.

Why Being Disliked is a Superpower (The Psychology of Rejection)

Psychologists have identified three core reasons we fear rejection:

1. **The Social Survival Instinct (Your Brain Thinks Rejection = Death)**

Humans evolved in tribes—being cast out once meant danger.

Your ancestors depended on group approval for food, shelter, and protection.

Your brain still treats rejection like a survival threat, even though today, it isn't.

This is why public criticism, social exclusion, or disagreement feels so intense.

Solution? Reprogram your brain to see rejection as harmless.

Action Step: The "What's the Worst That Can Happen?" Reframe

Next time you fear judgment, ask:

- "Will this kill me? No. So why am I afraid?"
- "What's the worst that can happen—and is it really that bad?"

Most of the time, rejection is just discomfort—not danger.

2. **The "Nice Person" Conditioning (Why We Feel Guilty for Being Ourselves)**

From childhood, you were taught to be "nice" and avoid conflict.

"Be polite. Don't upset people. Always be agreeable."

Society conditions us to prioritize likability over authenticity.

But the most successful, respected people? They are NOT universally liked.

Solution? Stop apologizing for who you are.

Action Step: The "Not Everyone Will Like Me—And That's Okay" Affirmation

1. Say out loud:
   "I accept that some people won't like me, and that's okay."
2. Repeat this daily until it feels normal.

Freedom begins when you stop needing approval.

3. **The Fear of Judgment (Why People's Opinions Seem Bigger Than They Are)**

You overestimate how much people care about you.

The Spotlight Effect (a proven psychological bias) makes you think everyone is watching.

In reality, most people are too busy thinking about themselves to analyze your every move.

The truth? People will judge you no matter what you do—so do what you want anyway.

Solution? Shrink the "Spotlight Effect."

Action Step: The "Nobody Cares" Mindset Shift

1. When self-doubt hits, remind yourself:
   "Most people won't remember this in a week."
   "I am free to live my life without their approval."

When you stop fearing judgment, you become unstoppable.

The 3-Step Fearless Mindset Framework

Want to stop fearing criticism? Follow this system:

Step 1: Detach – Stop Taking Rejection Personally

Step 2: Reframe – See Disapproval as a Filter, Not a Failure

Step 3: Own It – Fully Embrace Who You Are

STEP 1: Detach – Stop Taking Rejection Personally

The #1 Mistake: Thinking Someone's Opinion Defines You

Truth? What someone thinks of you is a reflection of them—not you.

If someone dislikes you, it's based on their beliefs, biases, and experiences.

Their reaction has more to do with them than with you.

Action Step: The "Is This My Truth?" Filter

When facing criticism, ask:

"Do I actually agree with this, or is this just their opinion?"

If it doesn't align with who you are, let it go.

STEP 2: Reframe – See Disapproval as a Filter, Not a Failure

Why Being Disliked is a Good Sign

Not everyone is meant to like you—this is how you find your true people.

Solution? See rejection as a filter, not a flaw.

Action Step: The "Not for Everyone" Rule

1. Accept that when some people dislike you, others will LOVE you for the same reason.

2. Instead of thinking "I must change to be liked," say: "I'd rather be real and attract the right people than be fake and please the wrong ones."

Rejection redirects you to where you truly belong.

STEP 3: Own It – Fully Embrace Who You Are

The Most Confident People Are the Ones Who Own Themselves

People admire those who don't apologize for who they are.

The most charismatic people? They embrace their quirks.

The most influential leaders? They don't seek approval—they set the standard.

Solution? Drop the need to explain yourself.

Action Step: The "Zero Justification Rule"

Next time you make a decision, don't explain or defend it.

If someone asks, "Why are you doing that?" → Answer with confidence.

Example: "Because I want to." No further explanation needed.

You don't owe anyone an explanation for being yourself.

Final Thoughts: The Freedom of Not Caring

What if you stopped worrying about being liked?

What if you lived for yourself instead of for approval?

What if you finally felt free?

The moment you embrace being disliked; you unlock unstoppable confidence.

The question is:

Are you ready to own your power?

Because once you do, the world adjusts to you—not the other way around.

* * *

20

The Art of Saying No

"The art of leadership is saying no, not saying yes. It is very easy to say yes."

— Tony Blair

* * *

Why Is It So Hard to Say No?

Let's be real.

- Have you ever said yes to something you didn't want to do—just to avoid disappointing someone?
- Have you ever felt guilty after setting a boundary?
- Have you ever overcommitted because saying no felt uncomfortable?

If so, you're not alone.

Your brain is wired to avoid conflict and seek approval.

- From childhood, you were taught to be agreeable and "nice."
- Society conditions us to put others' needs before our own.
- Your brain sees rejection as a threat—so it makes saying no feel risky.

But here's the truth: **Every time you say yes to something you don't want; you say no to yourself.**

This chapter will show you how to say no confidently—**without guilt, fear, or anxiety.**

* * *

Why We Struggle to Say No (The Psychology Behind It)

Psychologists have found that difficulty saying no comes from **three mental patterns:**

1. The Guilt Loop (Why We Feel Bad for Prioritizing Ourselves)

You've been conditioned to believe that saying no is selfish.

- *"Be helpful."*
- *"Good people always say yes."*
- *"If you say no, you'll disappoint others."*

Reality Check: Saying no isn't selfish—it's self-respect.

Action Step: The "Self-Permission Reframe"

Next time guilt creeps in, remind yourself:

- *"My needs matter too."*
- *"Saying no doesn't make me a bad person."*
- *"Protecting my time allows me to give my best when I do say yes."*

Boundaries are not rejection—they are a sign of self-worth.

* * *

2. The People-Pleasing Trap (Why We Fear Disapproval)

Humans evolved to seek social approval.

- In ancient times, being part of a tribe meant survival.
- Your brain still associates rejection with danger—even though today, it isn't.
- This is why saying no feels like you're risking relationships.

Solution? Rewire your response to disapproval.

Action Step: The "Respect Over Approval" Mindset

Shift your goal from seeking approval to earning respect.

- Instead of thinking *"Will they be mad?"* ask:
  "Do I respect myself for this decision?"

People respect those who value their time and energy.

* * *

3. The Overcommitment Cycle (Why We Say Yes Even When We Don't Want To)

Your brain underestimates future exhaustion.

- You say yes today, thinking, *"I'll have time for this later."*
- But when the time comes, you feel stressed, overwhelmed, and resentful.
- The pattern repeats—because you don't want to seem unreliable.

Solution? Pause before committing.

Action Step: The "Let Me Check My Calendar" Rule

- When asked for something, don't respond immediately.
- Say: *"Let me check my schedule and get back to you."*
- This gives you time to decide without pressure.

Most requests aren't urgent—take time before saying yes.

* * *

The 3-Step "Confident No" Framework

Want to say no without guilt? Follow this system:

- **Step 1:** Decide – Know Your Priorities First
- **Step 2:** Deliver – Say No Clearly and Confidently
- **Step 3:** Defend – Handle Pushback Without Guilt

* * *

STEP 1: Decide – Know Your Priorities First

The #1 Mistake: Saying Yes by Default

Truth? If you don't set your own priorities, someone else will.

- Every yes to something unimportant is a no to something meaningful.
- Successful people say no often—because they are clear on what matters.

Action Step: The "Priority Filter" Test

Before saying yes, ask:

- *"Does this align with my goals?"*
- *"Would I still say yes if this was happening tomorrow?"*

If the answer is no, decline with confidence.

* * *

STEP 2: Deliver – Say No Clearly and Confidently

How to Say No Without Feeling Awkward

Most people overexplain, apologize, or hesitate—making the no sound weak.

Solution? Keep it simple and firm.

Action Step: The "3 Versions of No" Script

1. **The Direct No:**
   "I appreciate the offer, but I have to decline."
2. **The Soft No:**
   "That sounds great, but I won't be able to commit right now."
3. **The Future No:**
   "I can't do it right now, but feel free to check in with me next time!"

No need to overexplain. Keep it short and confident.

* * *

STEP 3: Defend – Handle Pushback Without Guilt

What If Someone Won't Take No for an Answer?

- Some people will push back—expect it.
- They might guilt-trip you.
- They might try to negotiate.
- They might act disappointed.

Solution? Repeat, don't explain.

Action Step: The "Broken Record" Technique

If someone insists, don't give new reasons—just repeat your no.

- **Example:**
  "But I really need your help!"
  "I understand, but I still won't be able to."

People eventually back off when they see you're firm.

* * *

Final Thoughts: No is a Complete Sentence

What if you stopped saying yes out of guilt?

What if you protected your time like a billionaire?

What if you finally felt free?

The moment you master saying no, you reclaim control of your life.

The question is:

Are you ready to set boundaries with confidence?

Because once you do, you'll never feel trapped again.

* * *

21

How to Handle Failure & Rejection

"Success is stumbling from failure to failure with no loss of enthusiasm."

– Winston Churchill

* * *

Why Failure Feels So Painful

Let's be real.

Have you ever hesitated to try something new because you feared failing?

Have you ever felt like rejection was personal—like it meant you weren't good enough?

Have you ever let one setback make you doubt everything?

If so, you're not alone.

Your brain is wired to avoid failure.

Evolutionarily, humans needed to avoid mistakes—because in ancient times, failure often meant death.

Your brain still treats failure as a survival threat, triggering fear, anxiety, and self-doubt.

This is why rejection stings and why many people give up after just one setback.

But here's the truth: **Failure is not the opposite of success—it's part of it.**

This chapter will show you how to rewire your brain to embrace failure, handle rejection without emotional distress, and use setbacks as fuel for growth.

* * *

Why We Fear Failure (The Psychology Behind It)

Psychologists have found that our fear of failure comes from three core mental traps:

1. The "Fixed Identity" Trap (Why We Take Failure Personally)

Most people see failure as a reflection of their worth—rather than as an event.

- If you fail a test, you might think *"I'm not smart."*
- If you get rejected, you might think *"I'm not good enough."*
- If a business fails, you might think *"I'm not cut out for this."*

Reality Check: Failure is something you experience, not who you are.

Action Step: *The "Separate the Event from the Identity" Reframe*

- Next time you fail, say:

   o   *"This happened, but it doesn't define me."*
   o   *"Failure is an event, not a label."*

You are not your failures. You are what you do next.

* * *

2. The "All-or-Nothing" Fallacy (Why One Failure Feels Like the End)

Your brain exaggerates the consequences of failure.

- *"If I fail this exam, my career is over."*

- *"If this business idea flops, I'll never succeed in life."*
- *"If this relationship ends, I'll never find love again."*

Reality Check: One failure doesn't mean permanent failure.

Action Step: *The "Zoom Out" Perspective Shift*

- When you fail, ask:

  - *"Will this matter in 5 years?"*
  - *"Is this the only path to success, or just one of many?"*

Most failures are temporary detours, not dead ends.

* * *

3. The "Fear of Judgment" Loop (Why We Care What Others Think)

Most people fear failure not because of the failure itself—but because of what others will think.

- *"What if they laugh at me?"*
- *"What if people think I'm a loser?"*
- *"What if I embarrass myself?"*

Reality Check: People are too busy worrying about themselves to focus on your failures.

Action Step: *The "Nobody Cares as Much as You Think" Reminder*

- Ask yourself:

  - *"If someone else failed at this, would I judge them forever?"*

- Recognize that failure fades faster than you think.

Your failures are not the center of the universe. Move forward.

* * *

The 3-Step "Resilience Formula"

Want to bounce back from failure stronger than ever? Follow this system:

1. **Reframe – Change How You See Failure**
2. **Rebuild – Extract the Lessons & Adjust**
3. **Reignite – Use Failure as Fuel for Your Next Move**

* * *

STEP 1: Reframe – Change How You See Failure

The #1 Mistake: Seeing Failure as an Endpoint

Truth? Failure is not a stop sign—it's a stepping stone.

- Thomas Edison failed too many times before inventing the lightbulb.
- Walt Disney was fired for having "no creativity."
- J.K. Rowling was rejected 12 times before Harry Potter was published.

Action Step: *The "What Did This Teach Me?" Reframe*

- Instead of asking *"Why did I fail?"* ask:
    - *"What is this failure teaching me?"*
    - *"How can I use this lesson in my next attempt?"*

Failure isn't the enemy—stagnation is.

* * *

STEP 2: Rebuild – Extract the Lessons & Adjust

Why Successful People Fail Faster (and Better)

The faster you fail, the faster you learn.

Instead of fearing failure, successful people use it as data.

Every failure gives feedback—if you pay attention.

Solution? Build a system for extracting lessons from failure.

Action Step: *The "Failure Debrief" Method*

- After a setback, ask:
  - *"What worked?"*
  - *"What didn't work?"*
  - *"What will I do differently next time?"*

The difference between winners and losers? Winners learn and adjust.

* * *

STEP 3: Reignite – Use Failure as Fuel for Your Next Move

How to Turn Setbacks into Motivation

Failure is fuel—if you use it right.

- Michael Jordan was cut from his high school basketball team— he used it as motivation.
- Steve Jobs was fired from Apple—he came back and revolutionized the industry.

Solution? Convert failure into momentum.

Action Step: *The "Prove Yourself Right" Challenge*

1. Take your biggest failure and turn it into a goal.
2. Example: If you failed at a business, set a challenge: *"I will build a new business and make it profitable in 12 months."*
3. Use failure as motivation to prove yourself right.

The best revenge against failure? Massive success.

* * *

Final Thoughts: Fail Harder, Fail Smarter

What if you stopped fearing failure?

What if you saw rejection as redirection?

What if you used every setback as a stepping stone?

The moment you reframe failure, your entire life changes.

The question is:

Are you ready to fail forward?

Because once you do, nothing will ever hold you back again.

* * *

22

Building an Unshakable Mindset

"You cannot control what happens to you, but you can control your attitude toward what happens to you."

– Viktor Frankl

* * *

Why Do Some People Crumble While Others Rise?

Let's be real.

Have you ever felt mentally exhausted, unable to push forward?

Have you ever let stress, failure, or criticism shake your confidence?

Have you ever admired people who seem to handle anything life throws at them?

If so, you're not alone.

The truth is, mental toughness isn't something you're born with—it's something you build.

- Some people break under pressure because they see adversity as an attack.
- Others rise because they see adversity as a test—a chance to grow stronger.

The difference? Mindset.

This chapter will show you how to develop an unshakable mindset—one that thrives under pressure, turns stress into strength, and makes you unstoppable.

* * *

Why Your Mindset Determines Your Reality (The Science of Mental Toughness)

Psychologists have discovered that mental resilience is built through three core principles:

1. Cognitive Reframing (How You Interpret Challenges Matters More Than the Challenge Itself)

Your brain doesn't respond to reality—it responds to your perception of reality.

- If you see a challenge as a threat, your brain triggers fear and hesitation.
- If you see a challenge as an opportunity, your brain triggers motivation and focus.

Reality Check: The event itself doesn't define you—your interpretation does.

Action Step: The "What's the Gift in This?" Reframe

1. Next time you face a problem, ask:

- *"What is this teaching me?"*
- *"How can this make me stronger?"*

Your brain will always find what you focus on—train it to find strength, not weakness.

2. Emotional Regulation (Mastering Your Reactions Instead of Being Controlled by Them)

Unshakable people don't avoid emotions—they master them.

- Stress isn't bad—it's your reaction to stress that makes or breaks you.
- Fear isn't the enemy—it's how you respond to fear that defines success.

Solution? Train your brain to stay calm under pressure.

Action Step: The "Pause & Breathe" Method

1. The moment stress hits, take a deep breath.
2. Say to yourself:

   - *"This is just a feeling. I can handle it."*

Respond with clarity, not panic.

The strongest minds aren't the ones without emotions—they are the ones in control of them.

3. Stress Exposure (Why Comfort Zones Kill Mental Toughness)

Your brain is like a muscle—the more you expose it to stress, the stronger it gets.

- Navy SEALs train in extreme conditions so that real combat feels easier.
- Elite athletes push their limits daily so that competition feels natural.
- The most successful people seek discomfort—because it toughens the mind.

Solution? Train your mind by voluntarily facing discomfort.

Action Step: The "Controlled Adversity" Challenge

1. Choose one uncomfortable thing to do daily (cold showers, public speaking, early wake-ups).
2. Do it—even when it's hard.
3. Train your brain to see discomfort as growth, not pain.

Every time you push through discomfort, you rewire your brain for resilience.

* * *

The 3-Step "Unshakable Mindset" Framework

Want to develop mental toughness? Follow this system:

- **Step 1: Rewire – Upgrade Your Thinking Patterns**
- **Step 2: Rebuild – Strengthen Your Emotional Control**
- **Step 3: Reinforce – Train Your Brain for Long-Term Resilience**

* * *

STEP 1: Rewire – Upgrade Your Thinking Patterns

The #1 Mistake: Letting Negative Thoughts Control Your Actions

Truth? Your thoughts create your reality.

- If you think you're weak, you act weak.
- If you think you're strong, you act strong.

Action Step: The "Choose a Better Thought" Exercise

1. When self-doubt hits, ask:

   - *"Is this thought serving me?"*

2. If not, replace it with:

   - *"What's a stronger, more empowering thought?"*

Your thoughts are just suggestions. Choose the ones that serve you.

* * *

STEP 2: Rebuild – Strengthen Your Emotional Control

How to Stay Calm Under Pressure Like a Navy SEAL

Elite performers don't avoid stress—they train themselves to handle it better.

Solution? Use the same techniques as Navy SEALs and elite athletes.

Action Step: The "4x4 Breathing" Technique

1. In stressful moments, breathe in for 4 seconds, hold for 4, exhale for 4, hold for 4.
2. Repeat 3 times.

This technique instantly calms the nervous system—use it before big decisions.

* * *

STEP 3: Reinforce – Train Your Brain for Long-Term Resilience

Why Mental Toughness is Built, Not Born

The most mentally tough people weren't born that way—they trained for it.

Solution? Expose yourself to challenges daily.

Action Step: The "One Hard Thing a Day" Rule

1. Pick something slightly uncomfortable daily (a tough conversation, a new challenge, physical exercise).
2. Push through, even when your mind resists.

The more you do hard things, the easier they become.

* * *

Final Thoughts: Strength is a Choice

What if you stopped avoiding discomfort?

What if you trained your brain to see stress as fuel, not fear?

What if you became unshakable?

Your mind is your strongest asset—if you train it right.

The question is:

Are you ready to build a mindset that nothing can break?

Because once you do, life will never feel the same again.

* * *

23

The Science of Happiness & Fulfillment

"Happiness is not something ready-made. It comes from your own actions."

— Dalai Lama

* * *

Why Do So Many "Successful" People Feel Empty?

Let's be real.

- Have you ever thought that once you reached a certain goal, then you'd be happy?
- Have you ever achieved something big—only to feel strangely unfulfilled afterward?
- Have you ever wondered why some people seem effortlessly happy while others always chase it?

If so, you're not alone.

Most people are taught a flawed happiness formula:

"If I get the promotion, then I'll be happy."

"If I make more money, then I'll feel fulfilled."

"If I find the right relationship, then my life will feel complete."

But here's the truth: **Happiness isn't something you chase—it's something you cultivate.**

This chapter will show you the science of happiness, the mistakes that keep people stuck in unfulfillment, and how to build a deeply satisfying life.

* * *

Why We Struggle with Happiness (The Psychology Behind It)

Psychologists have identified three key reasons why happiness feels elusive:

* * *

The Hedonic Treadmill (Why Achievements Stop Feeling Exciting Over Time)

Your brain adapts to new highs—making them feel normal.

- You land your dream job, and at first, it feels amazing.
- A few months later, you start wanting something bigger.
- You hit a new milestone, but the excitement fades quickly.

Solution? Stop relying on external achievements for happiness.

Action Step: *The "Gratitude Reset" Method*

- Every morning, write down 3 things you appreciate about your current life.
- This rewires your brain to find happiness in the present—not just in the future.

Fulfillment doesn't come from getting more—it comes from appreciating what you have.

* * *

The "I'll Be Happy When..." Illusion (Why We Delay Joy for the Future)

Your brain tricks you into thinking happiness is always "one step away."

- *"Once I make six figures, I'll feel secure."*
- *"Once I get married, I'll finally be happy."*
- *"Once I retire, I'll finally enjoy life."*

Reality Check: If you can't find happiness now, you won't find it later.

Action Step: *The "Happiness Now" Experiment*

- Ask yourself: *"What would my ideal life look like if I already had everything I wanted?"*
- Find small ways to live that version now—before achieving the goal.

Happiness isn't a destination—it's a way of living.

* * *

The External Validation Trap (Why We Let Others Define Our Happiness)

Many people seek happiness through approval—but it never lasts.

- Social media tricks you into chasing likes, status, and comparisons.
- Society teaches you that happiness comes from "having more."
- But external validation creates temporary highs, not lasting fulfillment.

Solution? Detach your happiness from external sources.

Action Step: *The "Intrinsic Joy" Test*

- Ask yourself:
  "Would I still do this if no one knew about it?"
- If yes, it's a true source of happiness. If no, it's probably just external validation.

True fulfillment comes from doing what matters to you—not from impressing others.

* * *

The 3-Step "Fulfillment Formula"

Want to create deep, lasting happiness? Follow this system:

1. **Redefine – Shift Your Definition of Happiness**
2. **Rewire – Train Your Brain for Daily Fulfillment**
3. **Realign – Design a Life That Feeds Your Soul**

* * *

STEP 1: Redefine – Shift Your Definition of Happiness

The #1 Mistake: Thinking Happiness Comes from More

Truth? The happiest people don't have the most—they appreciate the most.

Studies show that beyond a certain income level, more money doesn't increase happiness.

The most fulfilled people focus on purpose, relationships, and personal growth.

Action Step: *The "What Actually Makes Me Happy?" Reflection*

- Make a list of times you felt truly happy.
- Identify common patterns—was it money, or was it moments, growth, and connection?

Once you know what truly brings joy, you can design your life around it.

* * *

STEP 2: Rewire – Train Your Brain for Daily Fulfillment

Why Happiness is a Habit, Not an Event

Your brain builds happiness through repeated actions, not one-time achievements.

Solution? Make joy a daily habit.

Action Step: *The "5-Minute Joy Practice"*

- Every day, do one small thing that brings you joy (listening to music, reading, nature walks).
- Over time, this rewires your brain to find happiness in everyday moments.

Happiness isn't found—it's built.

* * *

STEP 3: Realign – Design a Life That Feeds Your Soul

Why Purpose Creates the Deepest Happiness

Studies show that people who feel a sense of purpose report the highest levels of fulfillment.

- Happiness from pleasure is temporary.
- Happiness from meaning lasts.

Solution? Align your life with purpose.

Action Step: *The "Passion & Purpose Check"*

- Ask:
  "What would I do even if I wasn't paid for it?"
  "What energizes me instead of draining me?"
  - Prioritize these things in your daily life.

Fulfillment comes from doing what truly lights you up.

* * *

Final Thoughts: Happiness is a Skill, Not an Accident

What if you stopped chasing happiness and started creating it?

What if you found joy in the present instead of waiting for the future?

What if your fulfillment wasn't dependent on anything external?

The moment you stop seeking happiness outside yourself, you finally find it within.

The question is:

Are you ready to build a life of deep, lasting happiness?

Because once you do, everything changes.

* * *

24

The 1% Rule – How Small Habits Create Big Changes

"Small daily improvements are the key to staggering long-term results."

– James Clear

* * *

Why Big Changes Fail (And Tiny Changes Win)

The Illusion of Big Change

Imagine this: You decide it's time to transform your life. You set an ambitious goal—maybe it's running a marathon, launching a business, or losing a significant amount of weight. The first week, you're all in. By week two, the excitement fades. Before you know it, you're back to old habits, feeling defeated.

Sound familiar? You're not alone. Most people bite off more than they can chew, expecting massive results from massive effort. When the progress doesn't show up quickly, they burn out. But here's the secret: It's the small, consistent actions that deliver the biggest transformations over time.

* * *

The Power of Incremental Growth (The Kaizen Approach)

Ever heard of Kaizen? This Japanese philosophy focuses on steady, incremental improvements. Instead of trying to overhaul your life overnight, Kaizen teaches you to take manageable steps that build on each other. It's like putting money into a high-yield savings account. You might not see much at first, but given time, the results compound.

Key ideas:

- Improving by just 1% each day can lead to a 37x improvement over the course of a year.
- Small habits create momentum and build on themselves, like compound interest.
- Long-term consistency amplifies results.

What does this mean for you? Forget the dramatic overhauls. Focus on small, sustainable changes that feel almost too easy. When repeated daily, these tiny steps create massive, lasting shifts.

* * *

How Small Changes Rewire Your Brain

Your brain loves repetition. Motivation might get you started, but repetition is what makes habits stick. With every small action, you reinforce neural pathways. Over time, these actions become second nature. And that's the real magic of incremental improvement—it doesn't feel like effort anymore.

Try the "Two-Minute Rule":

When starting a new habit, make it ridiculously easy. Want to meditate? Start with just 10 seconds. Want to exercise? Begin with one push-up. Once you've started, it's easier to keep going. Momentum, not motivation, is the real key to change.

* * *

The Identity Shift: Small Wins, Big Confidence

The real power of small habits isn't just in the actions—it's in who you become. Each tiny success builds your confidence and reinforces a new identity. Write a single sentence every day, and soon you'll think of yourself as a writer. Do one push-up, and you're no longer someone who "never works out." Small wins change the way you see yourself.

Your new mantra:

Instead of saying, "I want to start writing," say, "I am a writer."

Instead of saying, "I want to get fit," say, "I am an athlete."

Shifting how you identify yourself is the first step toward meaningful transformation.

* * *

The 3-Step Framework for Growth

Step 1: Start Tiny

Lower the barrier to action. Too many people aim too high too soon and give up when it gets hard. The key is to make it almost effortless. Want to exercise? Start with one push-up. Want to meditate? Begin with 10 seconds. Once you're in motion, it's easier to keep going.

Step 2: Stay Consistent

A habit isn't built in a single day. It's the result of showing up regularly. At first, don't worry about intensity—focus on showing up. Once the habit is solid, you can gradually increase the effort.

Step 3: Trust the Process

Big results don't show up overnight. Most people quit when they don't see immediate progress. But the beauty of compounding is that it accelerates over time. Stay consistent, and you'll hit an inflection point where the results seem to appear out of nowhere.

* * *

Final Thoughts: Small Habits, Big Future

What if you stopped chasing massive overnight success and started focusing on small, consistent actions? What if, instead of looking for a quick fix, you trusted that tiny, daily improvements were reshaping your entire future?

The Kaizen mindset: Embrace the idea that success is the result of many small, steady steps. Before long, you'll look back and realize that those tiny actions created a life you once thought impossible.

* * *

25

The Flow State Formula

"Great things are done when men and mountains meet."

– William Blake

* * *

What If Productivity Felt Effortless?

You know that feeling. It's like stepping into a parallel dimension where time dissolves, everything clicks, and you're absolutely in the zone. You could be writing a report, climbing a rock face, or mixing the perfect cocktail of spices in your kitchen—it doesn't matter what the activity is. When you're in flow, it's as if the world fades away, and you're left with just you and the task at hand. Sounds amazing, right?

But let's get real. For most of us, that magical flow state feels elusive. You might stumble into it once in a while—usually by accident. The rest of the time? You're fighting off distractions, struggling to stay motivated, and wondering why some days feel like wading through molasses.

What if you didn't have to leave it up to chance? What if you could enter that productive, creative, fulfilling zone whenever you needed it?

* * *

What Is Flow? (The Science Behind It)

In the simplest terms, flow is when your mind is fully absorbed in an activity. Psychologists describe it as a "complete immersion" state—no room for overthinking, self-doubt, or mind-wandering. Neuroscientists have even pinpointed what's happening upstairs: certain brainwaves dominate, key chemicals flood your system, and your brain's default mode network (that chatty voice in your head) quiets down.

The trick to reaching flow is finding that Goldilocks zone of challenge and skill—not too easy (or you'll be bored), not too hard (or you'll give up). Think about it: the first time you rode a bike, it was a balancing act between "this is fun" and "I'm about to crash." Too easy, and you'd have stopped caring. Too hard, and you'd have quit. When it's just right, you lose track of time and feel completely "in it."

Action Step: Find Your Flow Sweet Spot

- Take your current project.
- Ask yourself: Is it way too easy, way too tough, or right on the edge of your abilities?
- If it's too easy, add a bit more complexity. If it's too hard, break it into smaller steps.
- The goal is to keep adjusting until you feel challenged, not crushed.

* * *

The 5 Neurochemicals of Flow (Why It Feels So Addictive)

Here's where it gets fun. Flow isn't just about being focused—it's also a neurochemical cocktail. The following brain chemicals surge when you're in flow:

- **Dopamine:** Keeps you motivated.
- **Norepinephrine:** Sharpens your attention.
- **Endorphins:** Make the process feel downright pleasurable.
- **Anandamide:** Enhances creative connections.
- **Serotonin:** Wraps things up with a satisfying post-flow glow.

Think of it like this: once you've experienced a great flow session, you'll want to come back for more. It's not just rewarding; it's addictive (in the best way).

Action Step: Create a Pre-Flow Ritual

- Find a simple activity that puts you in a good mood.
- It could be a 5-minute walk, a favorite playlist, or a quick stretching routine.
- Use this as your "warm-up" before diving into deep work.

* * *

The 3-Step Flow State Formula

Step 1: Eliminate – Remove What Blocks Flow

If you're juggling 12 things at once, you won't find flow. Multitasking is like trying to sprint while carrying a stack of plates. Instead, set aside a dedicated time for one task.

- **Action Step:** Block out 90 minutes of uninterrupted focus. Put your phone on silent, shut the door, and tell your brain, "This is our flow time."

Step 2: Activate – Use Flow Triggers to Enter the Zone

You can't force flow, but you can set the stage. Start by creating clear, specific goals. Make sure you're working on something challenging, but within reach.

- **Action Step:** Before starting, clearly define your outcome—like writing 500 words or solving one coding bug. Your brain needs a target to stay locked in.

Step 3: Sustain – Stay in Flow for Longer Periods

Once you're in flow, protect that state. Don't let every email ping or random thought yank you out. Gradually transition out of flow when the session ends—this helps you re-enter it more easily next time.

- **Action Step:** When you finish, take 5 minutes to reflect on what went well. Jot down one insight to carry into your next session.

* * *

Final Thoughts: Flow is Trainable

Flow doesn't have to be a lucky accident. It can be a repeatable part of your daily routine. By understanding the triggers and creating the right environment, you'll not only boost productivity—you'll rediscover the joy of doing great work.

* * *

26

Creating a Life Vision That Pulls You Forward

"When a man does not know what harbor he is making for, no wind is the right wind."

– Seneca

* * *

Why Most People Feel Stuck in Life

Let's be real.

Have you ever felt like you're working hard, but not really moving forward? Have you ever hit a goal, only to feel strangely empty afterward—like something vital was missing? If so, you're not alone.

Most people don't have a vision—they have a to-do list. And that's the problem. They spend their lives checking off random goals that don't lead anywhere meaningful. They chase short-term wins but never craft a long-term picture that excites them.

But here's the truth: motivation fades when your vision is unclear. It's like being on a treadmill—you're moving, but you're not going anywhere.

So, what if you could create a vision so compelling, it naturally pulls you forward—without needing constant discipline?

* * *

Why Most People Struggle with Long-Term Motivation (The Psychology of Vision)

Psychologists have found that long-term success isn't about sheer willpower—it's about clarity of purpose. Without that clarity, it's all too easy to drift, chase false goals, or keep waiting for the perfect moment to start.

1. The "Drifting" Problem (Why Most People Follow the Wrong Path)

Let's face it—most of us start life following someone else's roadmap. Maybe it's the script society handed us: "Go to school, get a job, retire." Or maybe it's the expectations of parents, teachers, or peers. But one day, we wake up and wonder, "How did I end up here?"

Solution:

Stop drifting and start designing.

- **Action Step:** Take five minutes to reflect. If you keep living the same way, where will you be in five years? If that doesn't excite you, it's time to redesign your path.

2. The "False Goals" Trap (Why Many People Feel Empty After Success)

This one's a killer. You achieve a big goal—land that job, buy that house, hit that milestone—only to feel a hollow kind of "is that it?" afterward. That's what happens when we chase goals that look good on paper, but don't align with our deeper values.

Solution:

Set goals that truly matter.

- **Action Step:** Write down three of your top goals. Now ask yourself: "If no one else knew I achieved these, would they still matter to me?" If the answer is no, you're probably chasing validation, not fulfillment.

3. The "Someday" Illusion (Why People Wait Too Long to Start Their Dream Life)

We've all told ourselves, "I'll get to it when things settle down." But here's the harsh truth: life never really "settles down." Waiting for the perfect time to start is just procrastination dressed up as planning.

Solution:

Stop waiting. Start small.

- **Action Step:** Pick one dream you've been putting off. Take one small step toward it today—even if it's just researching it online or spending 10 minutes sketching it out.

* * *

The 3-Step Life Vision Blueprint

Step 1: Define – Get Crystal Clear on What You Want

A vague vision isn't a vision—it's a wish. If you want something that motivates you every single day, you need clarity and detail.

- **Action Step:** Try the "Perfect Future" Visualization. Close your eyes and imagine your life five years from now. Picture everything—your surroundings, what you're doing, who's with you. Be as specific as possible, and write it down.

Step 2: Align – Ensure Your Daily Actions Match Your Vision

A powerful vision is useless if your daily habits pull you in the opposite direction. If your vision is to run a successful business, but you're spending all day on unimportant tasks, something's got to change.

- **Action Step:** Start with "Micro-Alignment." Pick one small habit that supports your vision—like reading a chapter of a business book or taking a short walk to clear your mind—and do it every day.

Step 3: Activate – Use Systems to Keep Momentum Alive

Motivation comes and goes, but systems stay. You need structures and reminders to keep you on track when the initial excitement fades.

- **Action Step:** Use "Vision Anchors." Write your vision on an index card or print it out. Keep it where you'll see it every day—next to your computer, on the fridge, or in your journal. Revisit it regularly, and set monthly check-ins to track your progress.

* * *

Final Thoughts: Your Future is Waiting

Imagine a life so exciting that you can't wait to wake up in the morning. Imagine a vision so compelling it fuels your actions without forcing yourself to "be disciplined." Imagine designing a future so inspiring that every step you take feels meaningful.

The moment you craft a vision that pulls you forward, everything changes.

The question is:

Are you ready to start creating the life you truly want?

* * *

27

Becoming the Architect of Your Own Life

"The best way to predict the future is to create it."

– Peter Drucker

* * *

Are You Living by Design or by Default?

Let's be real.

Have you ever felt like life was just happening to you, instead of you creating it? Have you ever looked around and realized that much of your life was shaped by other people's expectations?

I remember a time when I followed the script everyone else seemed to be reading from. Graduate from school, get a "respectable" job, keep my head down, and hope I'd eventually feel satisfied. But after a few years, I realized I was just going through the motions. I wasn't thriving—I was coasting.

Most people don't start out designing their lives. We begin by following the instructions handed to us—by family, by society, or by the invisible pressure to "fit in." If you're lucky, you eventually pause, look around, and think: *Wait a minute. Whose life am I actually living?*

And here's the truth: you are either the architect of your life, or you're just another character in someone else's story.

But the good news? You can pick up the pen and rewrite the script at any time.

* * *

Why Most People Stay Stuck (The Psychology of Passive Living)

So, why don't more people live intentionally? Psychologists have identified a few key reasons.

1. The "Autopilot" Trap

Have you ever driven somewhere and realized you couldn't remember the actual trip? That's autopilot—your brain loves efficiency, so it sticks to familiar patterns.

The same thing happens in life. Without noticing, you wake up, go to work, follow routines, and live out scripts that don't even excite you. Over time, it becomes the "default setting."

Solution? Interrupt the pattern.

Action Step: For the next 24 hours, question every action you take. Ask:

- "Am I doing this because I really want to—or just because it's what I've always done?"
  Identify one action you can change, right now, to break that pattern.

2. The "Permission" Myth

I used to think I needed someone else's approval before making big life changes. Maybe it was waiting for my boss's nod before starting a side project. Or waiting for my parents to say, "Sure, go for it!" when I wanted to switch careers.

But here's the reality: no one is coming to give you permission.

Solution? Give yourself the green light.

Action Step: Write down one thing you've been waiting to do until someone "allows" it. Cross out the excuse, and replace it with:

- "I give myself full permission to do this now."
  Then go take the first step.

3. The Fear of Change

Change is uncomfortable. Even when I was stuck in a job I didn't like, the thought of leaving felt terrifying. Why? Because it meant stepping into the unknown.

Your brain fears uncertainty—it clings to the familiar, even if the familiar isn't fulfilling.

Solution? Reframe your fear.

Action Step: Instead of fearing change, fear staying the same. Ask yourself:

- "If I don't change, where will I be in five years?"
  For me, that question was a game-changer. Staying stagnant became scarier than taking a risk.

* * *

The 3-Step Architect Framework

Step 1: Clear the Old Blueprint

If you're going to build something new, you can't start with a shaky foundation. Old beliefs, outdated habits, and borrowed goals have to go.

Action Step: Write down three beliefs or habits you've outgrown. For example:

- "I need everyone's approval to be successful."
- "I can't start a business until I'm perfectly ready."
- "Stability is more important than happiness."
  Cross them out, and replace them with beliefs that empower you.

Step 2: Design with Intention

Once you've cleared the old blueprint, it's time to create a vision that truly excites you.

Action Step: Write a bold vision of your life in five years. Be as specific as possible—where you live, what you do, who's with you, how you feel. Imagine the details so vividly that it makes you want to leap out of bed every morning.

Step 3: Build Daily

Big visions are great, but they can feel overwhelming if you try to do everything at once. The key is small, consistent steps.

Action Step: Commit to one small, bold action each day. Whether it's a five-minute habit, a quick email to a mentor, or researching that course you've been curious about—every small action adds up.

* * *

Final Thoughts: You Are the Architect

What if you stopped living by default and started designing your life on purpose?

What if every day felt aligned with your vision, rather than someone else's expectations?

The truth is, the moment you decide to become the architect of your own life, everything changes.

* * *

Conclusion: Reflect, Celebrate, and Continue the Journey

Congratulations on completing this journey! You've invested time, effort, and self-reflection into a transformation that goes beyond the pages of this workbook. By embracing solitude, you've not only learned to find peace in your own company but also uncovered a deeper sense of self-trust, resilience, and clarity.

As you look back, take pride in how far you've come. You've gained tools to manage emotions, confidence in making decisions independently, and a clearer sense of purpose. These aren't just short-term wins—they're stepping stones toward a more fulfilling life.

But transformation doesn't end here. The insights you've gained are seeds that will continue to grow. Keep nurturing them. Revisit the exercises that resonated most. Set new goals, push your boundaries, and stay connected to the lessons you've learned.

Remember:

- Your solitude is a strength, not a weakness.
- True confidence comes from within, not from others' approval.
- The habits and mindset shift you've developed can sustain your personal growth long-term.

You are now the architect of your own well-being. Keep designing, keep building, and keep thriving. You've proven you have the courage and discipline to transform your life. Now, let that transformation unfold in every area of your life moving forward.

30-Day Transformation Workbook

Welcome to your 30-day transformation workbook based on The Solitude Edge. This workbook is designed to help you embrace solitude, unlock your personal power, and master emotional resilience. It includes daily exercises, self-reflection prompts, and a scoring system to track progress.

How to Use This Workbook

Daily Exercises – Complete one exercise per day, aligned with key themes from the book.

Scoring System – Self-assess your progress using a scoring scale (1-10).

Before & After Analysis – Compare your results from Day 1 and Day 30 to track personal growth.

Day 1: Self-Assessment

Rate yourself (1 = Strongly Disagree, 10 = Strongly Agree):

I feel comfortable being alone. ______

I rely on external validation. ______

I manage my emotions effectively. ______

I have a clear sense of purpose. ______

I engage in deep, focused work without distractions. ______

I am confident in making decisions alone. ______

I practice self-discipline consistently. _____

Write down three intentions for this 30-day journey:

Days 2-29: Daily Exercises

Each day, complete the assigned task and reflect.

Week 1: Foundations of Solitude

Day 2: The Five-Minute Reset – Sit in silence for 5 minutes. Observe your thoughts without judgment.

Day 3: Identifying Noise – List three distractions in your daily life and ways to reduce them.

Day 4: Journaling for Clarity – Write one page about what solitude means to you.

Day 5: Breaking Free from External Validation – Spend a day making decisions without asking for outside opinions.

Day 6: Alone Time Challenge – Spend 30 minutes alone without digital devices.

Day 7: Deep Reflection – What emotions come up when you are alone? Write about them.

Week 2: Emotional Resilience & Mindset Shift

Day 8: Identify Your Fears – Write down three fears about being alone and reframe them positively.

Day 9: Mastering Self-Talk – Replace negative thoughts with empowering affirmations.

Day 10: Gratitude in Solitude – Write three things you appreciate about alone time.

Day 11: Decision-Making Test – Make an important decision without external influence.

Day 12: The Power of Creative Solitude – Engage in a solo creative activity (writing, painting, brainstorming).

Day 13: Overcoming Fear & Self-Doubt – Recall a moment of self-doubt and rewrite it as a lesson learned.

Day 14: Visualization Exercise – Close your eyes and visualize your ideal life in solitude.

Week 3: Deep Work & Productivity

Day 15: Digital Detox – Spend an entire day with minimal technology.

Day 16: Single-Tasking – Work deeply on one task without multitasking.

Day 17: Focus Score – Track how many minutes you worked without distraction.

Day 18: Journaling for Mental Clarity – Write about a decision you made while alone.

Day 19: The Art of Letting Go – Identify one limiting belief and replace it with a positive mindset.

Day 20: Identity Shifting – Write a letter to your future self, describing your growth.

Day 21: How to Handle Failure – Reframe a past failure using a guided exercise.

Week 4: Long-Term Transformation

Day 22: The Power of Saying No – Decline one unnecessary obligation.

Day 23: Social Detox – Avoid social media for a day and reflect on its impact.

Day 24: The 1% Rule – Make one small change that will compound over time.

Day 25: Entering Flow State – Track an activity where you lose sense of time.

Day 26: Building a Vision – Write a one-year vision statement for your life.

Day 27: Becoming the Architect of Your Life – List three ways you can design your ideal solitude practice.

Day 28: Reflection – What have you learned about yourself through this journey?

Day 29: Future Commitments – How will you maintain your solitude practice?

Day 30: Final Assessment & Growth Analysis

Re-rate yourself from Day 1. Have your scores improved?

I feel comfortable being alone. ______

I rely on external validation. ______

I manage my emotions effectively. ______

I have a clear sense of purpose. ______

I engage in deep, focused work without distractions. ______

I am confident in making decisions alone. ______

I practice self-discipline consistently. ______

Final Reflection Questions

What was the biggest insight you gained about solitude?

What challenges did you face, and how did you overcome them?

How do you feel different from when you started this workbook?

What habits will you continue beyond these 30 days?

Congratulations on completing your 30-day journey! You have now mastered the art of solitude and unlocked new levels of personal power. Keep going!